I've watched Andy grow over the last twenty years into a leader's leader. I know his heart; he's the real deal! This book will help any leader who will listen and learn and do what it says! There is good stuff in here for learners who long to be leaders!

—**Jim Wideman**
Children's Ministry Pioneer
President, Jim Wideman Ministries

This book provides an excellent overview of the practical side of children's ministry . . . Reading this book felt like a face-to-face conversation with the author. Including discussion questions at the end of each chapter also makes this book an excellent training tool to use with volunteers.

—**Judy Comstock**
Executive Director
International Network of Children's Ministry
Children's Pastors' Conference (CPC)

We have known Andy since his college days, and he has always had a passion for children's ministry . . . He is a man of passion, compassion, and dedication . . . This book will undoubtedly be a blessing and an encouragement to many who follow in his footsteps.

—**Dale VonSeggen**
Co-founder of One Way Street, Inc.

Once you pick up this book, you'll have a hard time setting it down . . . If you want to move your leadership to the next level, this book is for you. You will be challenged both personally and professionally.

—**Ryan Frank**
Executive Editor
K! Magazine

Andrew Ervin's unique language freedom adds humanness to the narrative. His biblical references add solidness to the contents . . . This book provides inspiration and challenge for churches and children's ministries' leadership to connect personally and corporately with Jesus Christ and to offer opportunities for children to do the same.

—**Lynda T. Boardman**
Retired Global Director
Children's Ministries International
Church of the Nazarene

P9-CFC-680

# BEST PRACTICES FOR CHILDREN'S MINISTRY

Andrew Ervin

BEACON HILL PRESS
OF KANSAS CITY

ISBN 978-0-8341-2556-8

Printed in the
United States of America

Cover Design: Doug Bennett
Interior Design: Sharon Page

10 9 8 7 6 5 4 3 2 1

# THIS BOOK IS DEDICATED TO

My wife, Sharon Facemire Ervin
Who is my best friend and supported me
every step of the way

My three children:
Grant Andrew, Amber Reedy, and Hannah Leigh

My parents, Don and Pat Ervin, who still live
in Hollywood, Maryland. Thank you for
your love and support.

My brother William (Bill) Ervin

The eight Senior Pastors who hired me and
gave me an opportunity to serve. Thanks for believing in me.
Aubrey Smith, Larry Cook, Larry Leonard, Quentin Caswell, Lynn Holmes,
Russ Long, Buddy & Gaye Marston

The Board of Directors of the Nazarene Children's Leadership Network
who have followed my lead.

The congregations, volunteers, and team leaders of
Salem Fields Community Church, Fredericksburg, VA;
Immanuel Church, Lansdale, PA; Memphis Calvary Church, Cordova, TN;
Crosspointe Church, Orlando, FL;
Bel Air Church of the Nazarene, Bel Air, MD;
Crossroads Church, Ellicott City, MD.

# CONTENTS

# ACKNOWLEDGMENTS

The author would like to thank his mentors:
Dr. Bayse (Uncle Bud) H. Reedy, Jr.
Mr. and Mrs. Dale and Liz Von Seggen
Mrs. Lynda T. Boardman
Thanks for speaking into my life and this book.

**Special Thanks** to my editor, Melissa K. Hammer, of Word Action
Your patience and encouragement were a huge blessing!

# FOREWORD

A call to ministry is both exciting and full of anxiety, and it is not for the faint of heart. It takes courage, commitment, initiative, perseverance, grace, and most importantly calling. Children's ministry leaders face an array of challenges. Planning to meet a range of developmental needs through programming and policy development, involves vision as well as nurturing relationships with volunteers, other staff members, parents, and children. Building and training a team to share the load is paramount, but this takes time and attention. Pulled in many directions, the responsibility is daunting and many times overwhelming. As leaders, it is difficult to navigate the waters of vulnerability. The key for a successful ministry is to know where to turn for support and direction.

A call to children's ministry in today's culture is rarely accompanied by an instructor with skin and a "How to" manual. Studying God's Word and Christ's ministry gives guidance and encouragement. Mentors and teachers who will be open and honest, sharing their successes and failures, are a real treasure. Someone who is willing to be vulnerable and invest time and energy in a mentoring relationship is a blessing.

In recent years, I had the privilege to serve on the board of directors of the Nazarene Children's Leadership Network (formerly known as the Nazarene Children's Pastors' Association). As chairman of the board, Andy Ervin brought an abundance of energy and enthusiasm to the task. His vision and direction is fueled by his passion to reach children and to grow those who minister with children and their families. He challenged complacency in the church and encouraged relevance. As a former educator, Andy possesses depth in his understanding of children and how they learn. He offers a perspective born from experience in a variety of ministry and educational settings. As an ordained children's pastor, Andy developed and led teams of lay ministers.

The bottom line is—Andy has been there. Years of experience in the local church and as a children's ministry consultant provided opportunities for Andy to impact multiple churches of various sizes across the country. He understands the needs of both the local church and the children's pastor. In this book, Andy openly shares his ministry journey and his heart with children's leaders who are seeking new ideas and encouragement. He invites the reader to join in his learning process to learn from his mistakes, struggles, and victories. Andy is open to revealing his trials, offering a rare glimpse into the vulnerable side of pastoral ministry. Through his personal reflective writing, there is a willingness to allow God's redemptive nature to work. Andy leads from the front.

As a pastor of children's pastors and leaders, Andy understands the value of team ministry. The format you will encounter in these chapters offers a leadership team the opportunity to intentionally discuss important issues and reexamine existing philosophies and methods. The transparent sharing gives permission to try new ways of ministry, even if imperfectly executed. Andy is willing to walk with leaders who want to be challenged. Each chapter offers the reader tough, probing questions designed to bring focus to mission and vision.

Andy carefully chose to address several critical areas for ministry to children. By walking through this narrative, you and your team will be challenged to consider a variety of ministry experiences. He has shared transparently from his heart. He writes like he leads, with passion to reach children with the Good News of Christ and to equip those who serve and lead them.

I am thankful for mentors and teachers who risk taking the lead and step out in faith. Andy is among those for whom I am thankful.

—Leslie Hart, Global Director
Children's Ministries International
Church of the Nazarene
lhart@nazarene.org

# INTRODUCTION

*Best Practices for Children's Ministry* is a "must-read" for everyone involved in children's ministry and for those considering children's ministry as a career. The author, Reverend Andrew Ervin, relates his personal ministry journey in a transparent, realistic fashion, giving excellent practical, theoretical, and theological advice.

Rev. Ervin's passion for excellence in children's ministry is woven into every chapter, balancing the desire for perfection with the realism of working with imperfect people and imperfect organization structures. He urges advocacy for children's ministry, and casts a critical eye on churches that see children as a "hook" to land new families for the church, but are unwilling to truly make children's ministry a financial and organizational priority.

He covers all the major bases in children's ministry, including engagement with the Holy Spirit, relevance to current culture, teamwork, encouragement, transparency, communication, vision casting, and commitment. Each chapter is followed by discussion questions that challenge the reader to "look in the mirror" and evaluate commitment, motivation, priorities, passion, leadership style, and other important aspects of successful children's ministry leadership.

You will be informed, blessed, challenged, and motivated by this book to be a true children's ministry leader by becoming "the person who develops teams of people who are passionate about creating fun environments that lead children to Jesus Christ." (This is the author's definition of a "children's minister" from Chapter 1.)

—Dale and Liz Von Seggen
  Co-Founders of One Way Street, Inc. and
  Ministry Resources International, Inc.
  Veteran Children's Pastors and Children's Ministry Speakers/Consultants
  www.daleandliz.com

# LEADERSHIP AND CHILDREN'S MINISTRY
## TIMES HAVE CHANGED

**"My times are in your hands."**
*—Psalm 31:15*a

There I was in 1990 In a basement fellowship hall. Vinyl-tiled floors, cinderblock walls, and 35 elementary children fidgeting in metal chairs finished off the environment of my very first experience as a children's pastor. Straight from commencement, I had arrived a few days earlier. What seemed like only hours had now passed, but it was Sunday morning and time for me to minister to this group of children. For the first time I heard "Pastor Andy" from people who were half my size and were missing several front teeth.

In a matter of days, I had transitioned from a dorm and campus life that included 500 young adults whose major concern was getting to class on time and the long line at the "dug-out" snack bar, to this exciting ministry. Now I faced the questions, "Why can't that child sit while I am telling a Bible story? Why is that parent in my personal bubble making me endure breath and conversation that were equally unenjoyable?" The beginning of this exciting ministry required a sharp learning curve. Let's face it. I thought I was prepared, but I quickly came to realize I knew very little about what I was doing.

Perhaps a similar experience helped you realize that your preparation was not equal to the task at hand. This can be a place of fear. It can also prove to be an opportunity for the Holy Spirit to engage the life of someone who is called to the ministry of the gospel of Jesus Christ. My reflection about those "early days" is a combination of memories that hold great passion and enthusiasm for a cause along with fear of jumping into the unknown. These memories have now come to serve me well as benchmarks on my life's journey. They reveal a desire to keep relevant but to cling to the lessons learned as I embarked on this road called ministry.

When I began my professional ministry as a children's pastor, my background

**These memories have now come to serve me well as benchmarks on my life's journey.**

served me well. In the small rural community of Hollywood, Maryland, at the age of 12, I knelt at the altar at the close of a revival service. That night, I accepted the call to minister to children. At the age of 14, God confirmed that call again at a time of re-commitment. My pastor, Joseph Hoopengardner, evangelists, and Sunday school teachers had a part in stirring up the environment for the Holy Spirit to work in the life of the son of a firefighter and teacher. Their messages of holiness of heart and passion for reaching people spilled over into my life.

My mother, the children's ministry director of our local church, provided a place for me to serve and to gain valuable experience as a Sunday school teacher. Also, I began a puppet ministry team that presented the message of God's love to children in places outside the walls of the church. These were venues as simple as coffee houses in church basements to full worship services and mid-week programs as far north as Philadelphia. By the age of 15, I had experience in teaching, evangelism, and management of peers. God was preparing me for the future He had planned.

As I entered college, I was encouraged by the religion department to start classes in education. There were few or no classes designed for training people to minister to children. During my first education class,

I received a letter about an internship at a large church. The opportunity was also with a puppet training ministry. I jumped at the chance and applied. A few months later, I was on an airplane traveling west of the Mississippi, visiting 22 states in 10 weeks. Through that church, its puppet team, and the children's pastor's vision to make ministry to children fun and exciting, windows began to open wide in my heart and mind as to what the Lord had in store for me. I began to read everything I could find on children's ministry. In comparison to the resources available in the 21st century, that was very little. The idea of being a children's pastor had settled in my soul with a desire to make that my personal mission.

So now, return with me to that basement fellowship hall. I began this journey with a boom box, cassette tapes, an overhead projector, and pictures stuck to the wall. My weekly focus primarily hinged on preparing for one hour of children's worship and one hour on Wednesday night, so the choir could practice without children in the room. The bottom line: I created two programs a week. Now jump forward 20 years. The reality is, regardless of the church size and geographical location in the world, that simply does not "cut it" today.

I was fortunate that I was given the opportunity to grow with the ministry. Not

**I began to read everything I could find on children's ministry.**

everyone has a congregation that will let them "cut their teeth." Looking back over the years, I had a heart for ministry, education, and could manage groups of children, but I was clueless in understanding the leadership dynamics.

**Times have changed.**

No longer does doing programs become the summation of children's ministry in today's church. There is far more required and expected of children's ministry leaders. The role of children's pastor is much more complex. The expectations of children's ministry leaders have changed. Here are some subtle and some not so subtle changes that have occurred in the last two decades:

> The role of the children's pastor is much more complex.

- *Growing in knowledge of theology and human growth and development.* The ability to take biblical knowledge and content and structure it to the real life of a child with age-level appropriateness is essential. There must be personal confidence in knowing the growth patterns and cognitive abilities of children. A curriculum is a good and helpful tool but should not be the driving force. The driving force must come from the heart of God. The role of a God-called children's ministry leader is to follow the heart of God in relationship with children.

- **Fostering strong relationship skills.** Connecting with children is important, but connecting with parents and every age group in the church is also essential. This leads the way for intergenerational ministry and keeps children's ministries in the center of the congregation's vision. People do not value what they do not understand or cannot see as relevant. People will serve in children's ministries when they connect with its leader and that leader's passion. When you value others, your cause becomes their cause.

- **Developing a clear understanding of self.** Knowing how you as a leader are gifted and designed by your Creator is an absolute requirement. This paves the way for focusing on strengths rather than toiling away at weak areas that will produce few results.

- **Having a willingness to work with the imperfect organizational structure of the local church.** I love the Church. It has given me a place to serve. I have found it is the local church where my gifts have been best utilized. It has also been a place for my greatest challenges personally and professionally. Being a part of a church staff is not singing praise

I have found it is the local church where my gifts have been best utilized.

songs and praying out loud all day long. It is simply a place where human beings called by God are still working on their stuff. In essence: the mess of the human condition still exists even after you walk through the church office doors. You are continuing to grow while working through attitudes and speaking the truth in love.

- *Realizing that children and parents both need you.* There is no doubt that family life is the most critical need in our culture today. Globally, it is this need for ministry that reaches families that is vital for the future. We cannot wait for what has become a crisis to get worse before we treat it realistically. Partnering with parents is the way to lead children's ministries. Strong marriages mean strong families. Team up with people who parent well and learn from them.
- *Recognizing that the* post–9/11 *world needs advocates for children and children's ministry.* In a world where the threats of terrorism, hunger, poverty, disease, and abuse run wild, advocacy for children in your community is important. Whether you minister in a rural, urban, or suburban setting, there is the need

for and a call for safety and care for children. Often, these needs are overlooked, even in the church, due to budget cuts and adult-driven priorities. Put children first and foremost on agendas and community issues so their needs will be heard and addressed.

People need to be advocates for children and for children's ministry. The local church needs people to articulate the need for funding and resources for the ministry to children.

• *Working hard at communication.* People want to be part of something bigger than themselves. In order to develop teams, communicate what value they will receive from serving. This becomes an art form involving the style and personality of the children's pastor. In other words, there is no such thing as over-communicating. Use whatever technology is available. Websites, blogs, social networking utilities, and organizational networks are a great help in communicating concepts. A key to this is the development of leaders who have an emotional and spiritual stake in the bigger plan.

It is not surprising that expectations in the local church have changed. Church leaders and congregations are more aware of the allure children's ministries has to the community. Often, they make the mistake of referring to children as "bait" to get the parents to come. George Barna, in his book *Transforming Children into Spiritual Champions,* shares his research from churches that were surveyed. Children's ministry was important to them, but more money was spent on landscaping compared to the economic and human resources spent on ministry to children. Sadly, this means that a children's pastor is faced with creating ministry experiences without the benefit of adequate resources. This challenge needs to be heard by all church leaders as children's ministries' leaders are developed and given roles of leadership in the local church.

Take a look at this excerpt from a job posting a local church placed on a blog for attracting a new children's pastor:

> We want our new children's pastor to be creative, coachable, energetic, experienced in production, emotionally intelligent, connects with kids, connects with parents, connects with volunteers, sound biblical worldview, ability to teach, team-builder, relevant, cross-generational minded, team player, family orientated, technology adept, politically savvy, and juggle.

Is there a human being alive who could meet this local church's expectations? Do the people who wrote this job description

**Often they make**

**the mistake of**

**referring to children**

**as "bait" to get the**

**parents to come.**

need to re-think what they are asking for? Perhaps there is a need for a reality assessment in the establishment of a role for the children's pastor.

Often, I have been asked by a guest walking through the church door or a person in the community, "What do you do?" My standard answer to this question is, "I am the children's pastor." The usual response is, "Oh, that's nice," or "Wow, I thought you just volunteered," or even better yet, "So you have been in childcare for a while?"

May I test drive a new response I have been working on? Here it goes: "I am the person who develops teams of people who are passionate about creating fun environments that lead children to Jesus." What might be the response to this description?

Bottom Line: The church needs children's ministry leaders. Does that describe you? Are you hungry for a ministry that has a huge impact for generations? The local church can benefit from a children's ministry that connects with the overall vision and mission of the Church of Jesus Christ and the church that is carrying it out. A children's ministries leader who is a vision caster is needed, so that people will be inspired to follow. Too often this is not seen. Too often the call is ignored. But we must realize that when leadership is present and inspired by God, people will respond, fol-

**I am the person**

**who develops**

**teams of people**

**who are passionate**

**about creating**

**fun environments**

**that lead children**

**to Jesus.**

low, and become leaders involved in the vision and mission.

## Discussion Questions

1. Describe the journey that brought you to this point of leadership in children's ministries.

2. How has your heart changed during this time?

3. What do you see that has changed in how you approach your leadership in ministry?

4. In what areas have you grown stronger? What areas are still weak?

5. Do you know someone that you could share this with who would offer good feedback? Who is discipling you? Who is a mentor in your life and ministry?

# COMMUNICATING UP, DOWN, AND ALL AROUND
## THE ART OF VISION CASTING

**"Then Samuel said,
'Speak, for your servant is listening.'"—**
*1 Samuel 3:10*b

My fascination with the genre of science fiction came during my college years. As the popular series of the 1960's Star Trek made its come back in Star Trek: The Next Generation, I was intrigued with Mr. Spock and Vulcan characters who could communicate with others using an exercise called a Vulcan mind meld. This always looked so easy to do. Simply take your fingers and spread them out across a person's face and then firmly press and hold. Wah-la! Instant communication—the other person got it! How many nights have I lain awake wondering if people in a meeting I was leading "got it?" Or, if the person reading my proposal

COMMUNICATING UP, DOWN, AND ALL AROUND

was able to get all the passion and energy that was represented by that document? It is these kinds of questions that can motivate a children's ministry leader to play the mental tapes over and over and constantly self-evaluate, "Did I make that clear?"

Clarity in ministry is the result of understanding communication. It is the leaders who know their vision, and then transport it to the understanding of those God has placed in their sphere of influence, that have a clear ministry message. As a leader, you will begin by planning how and what will go into this very intentional set of messages. I like to think of it as 360 degree communication that begins and ends with you. This becomes your hook, line, and sinker. Let me explain:

**Hook:** What are the unique aspects of the vision that God has given you for your children's ministry?

- Biblically-based
- Fits with your SHAPE (spiritual gifts, heart, abilities, personality, and experiences)
- Fits the culture inside and outside the church

Ask yourself, "What is the vision God has given me for my children's ministries?"

**Line:** There are seven levels of communication for vision casting.

**Clarity in ministry is the result of understanding communication**

The Crowd/Community
The Congregation/Whole
All Volunteers/CORE
Your Leaders
Key Lay Leadership
Accountability/Staff
Lead Pastor(s)
You

This inverted pyramid concept places the emphasis on communicating completely around you. As the children's ministry leader, you have the key role to build your leadership and your communication with the entire staff and congregation, working your way up through the communication channels. This type of complete communication is vital when you want people to follow your leadership.

*Sinker:* Plan to revisit and recast your vision.
- Tell the stories again and again
- Develop and communicate a marketing plan so others can share in the vision

The success of this form of vision casting requires a lot of the children's ministry leader. This is you. This cannot be formulated "on the way to church" or "in the shower before a meeting." It requires purposefully planning, sharing, implementing, and revisiting the vision to accomplish the mission of children's ministry. This is ongoing, but you can follow these steps to set it in motion:

1. **Seek God's direction for vision.** This gives you, as the leader, the confidence to speak your vision boldly and with confidence. Any vision from God is going to be in harmony with the Word of God, the calling God has given to you, and the overarching vision of the place where you are serving. If none of these are the case, then you may want to reevaluate, abandon that particular vision, and go back and spend more time talking with God.

2. **Schedule time to meet with your lead pastor or pastors.** This should be a private time where you can focus. Get away from emails, mobile phones, and other distractions. Lead pastors are the God-given true litmus test for your children's ministry vision. If they agree with the direction and concepts, then you know it will harmonize with the rest of the church. This is the dream of healthy leaders today. They want their staff teams to take initiative.

Lead pastors are

the God-given

true litmus test

for your children's

ministry vision.

They want their team to come forward when something is burning inside them. Passionate leaders create an environment for passion to be nurtured and to grow into great things for God. Unhealthy leaders micro-manage and actually discourage initiative-taking team members. Teams will think, "Why bother, I just get shot down." If you do not have the kind of healthy relationship with your leader to have this level of communication, you may need to ask, "What is it about me (not your lead pastors) that needs to change in order for God's work to happen?"

3. **Get immediate supervisors or leaders on board with you.** Have a detailed approach. Be sure to have churned and crunched some finances or other resources to show the benefits of this investment. As children's pastors, always be ready to advocate for investing in the lives of children both in the church and the community. This is always a great need within any organization especially a church.

4. **Set a time to meet with fellow staff members and key lay leaders.** Communicate the value of the project. A good emphasis here is on assurances of roles. This way conflict does not arise with anyone due to a role

dilemma. Coworkers always look for options of supporting you while at the same time concentrating on their own tasks at hand. Clearly communicated plans will offer assurance and gain the trust of your coworkers and key leaders. After all, no one really likes surprises.

5. Then comes the real fun. **Take it to the congregation and crowd**. If a church-wide venue is not available, consider a newsletter or email blast that goes to everyone. This is where the vision must be the clearest and where the greatest potential for buy-in occurs. When everyone buys in to the plan for children's ministries, it could lead to a higher level of volunteerism.

6. Next, the eyes will be focused on you as you **implement the vision you communicated with the people around you.** Be specific in your time lines and communicate any changes, so you keep the credibility and trust of the people around you. When you achieve it, then celebrate with the whole church. Use this as encouragement that the kingdom of God is growing due to the communication and implementation of the vision God has given.

> Clearly communicated plans will offer assurance and gain the trust of your co-workers and key leaders.

So go ahead and listen, and you will hear what God has uniquely prepared for you! Trust it. Take a jump.

Paul writes to the early risk-takers in the church these words:

"Is there any encouragement from belonging to Christ? Any comfort from his love? Any fellowship together in the Spirit? Are your hearts tender and sympathetic? Then make me truly happy by agreeing wholeheartedly with each other, loving one another, and working together with one heart and purpose," (Philippians 2:1-2, NLT).

When you have everyone on board with your vision then you will find that conversations and planning fall into place. There will be a rhythm that emerges out of your vision. Ministry goes from being something that you need to defend to something that creates freedom. Often I had a volunteer come to me and say, "Andy, I get what you are trying to do with this." What a warm feeling that brings to the heart of any leader when the people surrounding the vision get it.

By now you are probably thinking that I am a verbal processor. You would be right, I am. My history with oral communication dates back to the late 1960s when it seemed to my parents that I was never going to speak but then one day it just happened. I spoke. Not unusual for a toddler's cognitive journey, some are just delayed. However, in the Ervin home it was always said, "Yup, that Andy, he was late starting to talk but once he did he never stopped."

But being highly verbal is sometimes overstated and the Bible gives us a clear message about how in the kingdom, God can use people at various levels of communication skill.

"Moses said to the LORD, 'O LORD, I have never been eloquent, neither in the past nor since you have spoken to your servant. I am slow of speech and tongue.' The LORD said to him, 'Who gave man his mouth? Who makes him deaf or mute? Who gives him sight or makes him blind? Is it not I, the LORD? Now go; I will help you speak and will teach you what to say," *(Exodus 4:10-12).*

Moses was a great leader with a speech disorder. Despite his stuttering, he communicated. Despite his lack of speed articulating, he led. Maybe this example is a reminder for all of us that heart trumps skill in many kingdom events. Moses also utilized the people around him. Aaron was the mouthpiece but did not replace the passion and zeal of his brother. To do so would have been disastrous for the people of Israel. Could it be that we need to learn ways to speak from the heart? Open a new conduit of communication through prayer that will allow the vision that God has given

**Could it be that**

**we need to learn**

**ways to speak**

**from the heart?**

you for your children's ministry to emerge and resonate with the people in your congregation. Lead, but also look to those around you to join you in leadership.

Whenever I would do a video shoot for promotion or vision casting I always looked for people who could speak from the heart. That was not to replace my voice or leadership, but it was designed to enhance it. You discover that those volunteers who get it provide a mouthpiece for further communication into the fiber of the community. People relate to what they are hearing and seeing and they become engaged and connected to the vision. It says: "There is room for me in this." However, the challenge will be: "What do I do with them after they connect?" Uh oh! Sounds like there is a need for a plan! Uh, right, you do need a plan! Keep reading.

## Discussion Questions:

1. When was the last time you heard from the Lord regarding the direction of your ministry?

2. If you are not a good communicator how can you improve? Who around you can help?

3. What personal experiences could you use to share with others when conveying vision?

4. What is your plan and timeline for communicating vision?

# IT'S ALL ABOUT TEAMWORK!

"Two are better than one, because they have a good return for their work: If one falls down, his friend can help him up. But pity the man who falls and has no one to help him up! Also, if two lie down together, they will keep warm. But how can one keep warm alone? Though one may be overpowered, two can defend themselves. A cord of three strands is not quickly broken."
—*Ecclesiastes 4:9-12*

After four years of successfully teaching fifth grade in public school I made a decision to interview in another school district. Little did I know at the time it would be a decision that would initiate tremendous obstacles and challenges such as I had never faced.

In 1990 I began teaching at Northfield Elementary School in Ellicott City, Maryland. It had been the flagship elementary school in that district for several years. The school was designed with the open classroom philosophy with classrooms that were spacious with very few walls and no doors. Learning centers were scattered all over the instructional area. Centers with headphones where children worked at what was called machine spelling where they heard a word, saw the word, and then wrote the word. We were very interactive as teachers. We switched classrooms and taught each others' classes for shared subject matter. I was one of five teachers who came together to teach in Team V. When one of us made pilgrim people we all did. There was mutual respect and cooperation with other educators. We trusted each other. That created an environment where we could celebrate the good and share the burden of the difficult. The 125 children in that grade level had the same shared educational experience.

Now get this! When I resigned that teaching position it was because we had moved to the other side of Baltimore and the one hour commute to teach was getting old. My own children never saw me. So I accepted a position at a school closer to our new home and church. From the onset it was a total 180 degree turnaround.

I moved from an open classroom to a traditional format: one room, a door, and the expectation that I teach all the subjects, all day to the same 35 kids. For the first few weeks of September that year I enjoyed the walls and the ability to close the door for a quieter feel during a test or during oral reading. However, the environment began to get stale when there was no variety and I was the solo instructor. You can imagine how this led to boredom, frustration, and finally to disciplinary issues such as a student throwing a ballpoint pen into the ceiling fan nearly blinding another student. Fun, right? Wrong.

At the time I did not see this contrast at work in my life and the educational adaptation that I was struggling to achieve. Bottom Line: It just felt like failure. But here is what I came to understand later about myself: *I am wired for teamwork.* And guess what? I am not alone. God has wired people for teamwork.

And the very sad reality is that when I arrive on the scene as the new children's pastor, I walk in the door knowing full well that there is an underlying wish of the church leadership that I simply fix everything. (After all isn't that why we hire in the church?) This is a lonely place to be. The same thing is there every time that you find people who feel alone, discouraged, unhappy, and frustrated. It is because they are lacking

**It is because they are lacking the fulfillment of one essential human need: TEAM.**

the fulfillment of one essential human need: **TEAM.** They feel alone. They need the support and camaraderie of others.

Bill Hybels, founding pastor of Willow Creek Community Church, said in his book, *Volunteer Revolution* that at one point Willow Creek could not get people to volunteer to cut the grass on the church property. They had good tools and equipment, even a riding mower, but there was no motivation or passion for the task. Then they decided to buy several riding mowers and they never had the problem again. Why? The volunteer grass cutters would circle their mowers, come together to share and pray, and then after a while they developed a bond. They became a **TEAM.** They had a shared support and passion for the task they were doing.

**Teamwork is a must.**

Craig Jutila, founder of Empowering Kids and former children's pastor at Saddleback Church stated in his book, *Leadership Essentials for Children's Ministry,* that teamwork requires five things:

- Cooperation
- Flexibility
- Commitment
- Loyalty
- Encouragement

*Cooperation* means that you have to work together. Your children's ministry must function as a co-op. It needs to operate with the idea that everyone has value and is an important part of the whole. Paul's analogy in 1 Corinthians 12:12-31 is of the body of Christ. He uses imagery of a physical body and how the body requires equal attention given to the eye as to the elbow. Both are needed. Both would be greatly missed. This is the same for the church as the body of Christ. If there are people who are just standing around in the back of children's church sipping coffee, chances are they will not be there very long. Make sure they understand their function, and then let them do it.

*Flexibility* can be described basically as: I can flex with my abilities. It cannot be all about me. If it is all about an individual or individuals then it is going to be "crash and burn" time. For example, the statement: "I only work with third graders" should be a good indicator that this person may not be a team player. Talk further. If the person proves inflexible, help the person find another ministry. People who serve in children's ministry need be able to go with the flow. The needs can change from one week to the next so teams have to adjust and compensate.

*Commitment* is a huge deficit in the church and today's culture. We have allowed technology and consumerism to infiltrate our hearts to the point that when conflict does arise we just dispose of relationships. Some of the best friendships I have came out of pain and a desire to grow through the issues rather than just walk away. It breaks my heart to have someone come and tell me that a leader or volunteer wants to quit or not even attend worship due to the guilt of walking away from a commitment. Why can't we create a culture within the church where we come to each other in truth and say, "I'm hurting" or "I need a break?" Instead there is silence and fear. As a leader, God is calling you to a higher level. Let's keep our commitments, and then strive to help others do the same.

*Loyalty* is tricky for it can be grossly misinterpreted. Loyalty does not mean that I am going to agree with everything that the team wants to do. Simply put, loyalty is working alongside the rest of the team to complete the goals or tasks regardless if I thought there was a better way. It means I hold up other team members even when I don't see eye to eye with every detail. Compromise can be healthy to the team if there is a sense that we all want the best for each other. Like trust, loyalty does not come automatically. Some leaders fail to realize that loyalty has to be nurtured and seasoned with cooperation and flexibility. The leader sets the tone for this in the model of teamwork that is implemented and encouraged.

*Encouragement* is the icing on the cake of teamwork. It is so vital to finding the

> Some of the best friendships I have came out of pain and a desire to grow through the issues rather than just walk away.

sweet part of the project or experience. People who are spiritually gifted with exhortation find this extremely easy, but every leader needs to be an encourager. This is regardless of the spiritual gifting. My grandmother made incredible carrot cakes. They were my Uncle Bud's favorite dessert. I remember watching Grandma take that cake and pour the cream cheese icing on it and then spread it out. Grandma did not waste any of that icing for she lavished it so thick on that cake. She made the cake special with her generosity. That is how we need to treat other team members. Give them preference. Lavish encouragement on them like that cream cheese frosting. It will build them up rather than tear them down. Find out what their favorite things are: candy bar, restaurant, genre of paperbacks, favorite food—and lavish those little tokens of encouragement on them. Be generous in your encouragement.

So how do you build these ministry teams? Any volunteer strategy that is worth the paper it is written on **must** include team development. For it is in this framework that basic human needs are met. There is nurture, there is trust, there is connection, and there is nourishment. Have you ever noticed that you are always at church for the meal times? You have to eat! Hey this is children's ministry! You must have snacks at those team meetings! But remember that feeding includes the spirit as well as the body.

This is the five step strategy that has worked well in the places I have had the opportunity to lead. Use this strategy to develop strong leaders in your children's ministry:

1. **Invite volunteers.** Make it personal, face to face, shoulder tap, follow the leading of the Holy Spirit to guide you to these encounters. (If you are an introvert I know you are going to shy away from this, but you have to do this to lead your children's ministry.)

   **Need fulfilled: To feel included and a part of something. To develop a sense of belonging.**

2. **Inspire volunteers to take a jump.** Encourage them to show up that next weekend and give it a try. Let them come and observe, walk around, and get a feel. Assign no specific responsibility yet. Afterward have them fill out your ministry application, background check forms, and submit references for you to check. This works better when they are motivated to be a part of your ministry. The returns on this are much higher if they have already caught your vision.

   **Need fulfilled: To take a risk, be vulnerable and learn something about themselves.**

3. **Place volunteers on a team.** A new volunteer is placed with a seasoned leader and they work together. Relationships and synergy grow, as before long they are doing ministry together. This connection keeps them on board with the vision and mission of children's ministry.
**Need fulfilled: To develop friendship and ministry support.**

4. **Give volunteers the opportunity to become a team leader.** Over time a volunteer grows into a team leader. Give the team leader increasing opportunity to lead, and to expand a focused ministry team. The team leader brings to the mix a unique and personal style of leadership that attracts others. These others may be people that would not have been seen or considered for ministry. Your net gets bigger to catch more volunteers as you expand your leadership team.
**Need fulfilled: To invest and to take ownership in the ministry.**

5. **Provide regularly scheduled planning and support.** Meet with your team leaders monthly to maintain a connection. Spend a portion of that time doing training and development.

> **The team leader brings to the mix a unique and personal style of leadership that attracts others.**

Sometimes this may mean purchasing a book and reading it together. Then during each monthly meeting spend time discussing the book, chapter by chapter. Another possibility is a leadership development series, such as John Maxwell's DVDs. His series have proven to be very well done and effective in providing leadership principles to ministry in the body of Christ. The point I want to make is that as the children's ministry leader it is your responsibility to help your team leaders grow. Give them the tools and empowerment that as they grow in training and knowledge, then they can grow the volunteers on their teams.

**Need fulfilled: To grow in leadership and ministry commitment and responsibility.**

*"In any organization people are only your greatest asset if you develop them."*
*—John Maxwell*

## Discussion Questions:

1. What would it take for you to go from being a recruiter to a team builder?

2. What fear do you have in approaching people?

3. What items on your team development plan have worked for you in the past?

4. What else are you being convicted about regarding your ministry volunteers?

It is important to give careful consideration to those you choose for ministry leadership. Remember to pray before saying anything to anyone. The Holy Spirit will hear you and guide you to the next great leader for children's ministry.

# THE ART OF DEVELOPING VOLUNTEERS
## BUT CALL THEM LEADERS!

**"For we are God's workmanship, created in Christ, Jesus to do good works, which God prepared in advance for us to do."**
*—Ephesians 2:10*

I had some really great professors in college. What a blessing it is to look back and see how they intentionally molded and directed the steps I took as a student, and then as a student teacher. I remember some of the content of their classes but mostly recall their voice, their warmth, and their encouragement. How fortunate I was to have many people involved in Andy Ervin's personal development plan.

My son, Grant, is a storyteller and an artist. That was evident even in his early elementary years. I would visit him in school at lunch and to my surprise I would be greeted by other children very anxious to ask questions like: "Mr. Ervin, were you in a rock band?" I'm sure my look was that of a perplexed parent. Then I would look over at a familiar face that was grinning from ear to ear. Something early on motivated this young boy of mine to use his imagination in ways that did not always seem normal: mustard on his pizza, folders of sketches stacked high, and later on taking a white canvas and creating such a compelling, thought-provoking painting of a werewolf eating a piece of popcorn from the view of the inside of his mouth. Did I mention this is video game art? I get so amazed at how an artist or storyteller can take nothing and turn it into something.

When it comes to developing volunteers (start calling them leaders—that keeps the bar raised high!) the good thing is that God has already made them. They are already special. Your job is to help them uncover their hidden talents. You see, in your church community you may have the very person that you need but their abilities are as yet undiscovered or untapped. In this way you need to see yourself not as a recruiter but as a talent treasure hunter.

The church, like most human institutions, works very hard at making development an assembly line process rather than encouraging uniqueness and individuality. So we buy a curriculum. We recruit a warm body and place them in a room with children and say, "OK, here you go, and have fun with that." Then return to collect the offering and attendance folder that was pushed under the door hoping that we don't hear any screaming. Having said that, let's not be too hard on the day-to-day church ministry environment. It really does mean well. The people really do mean well. There are times that it just gets caught in the same demands of time and resources that we all face. A basic truth: developing your volunteers takes time. The best part is that you can have fun doing it, and you can do it knowing that this is God-ordained ministry. It is His church!

If your children's ministry is going to have a growing number of leaders, here are some fun and easy things to do to create an environment for discovering these talented people.

**Start a new ministry.**

Look at your children's ministry and within this greater ministry start a new ministry. It could be offering prayer partnerships, (where you share prayer requests monthly with a group of prayer partners), a new type of worship venue, a new midweek small group, or a new type of community outreach event. When you start a new ministry you are giving your church an opportunity to see a fresh perspective on children's ministry. A new method attracts people and inspires. In doing this you are creating a broader net to catch new talents that are out there.

**Visit a new member's class.**

This is a place to get "fresh meat," actually I mean new leaders. Have a postcard with a simple overview of your ministry's opportunities, and then remember that you need to get their contact information. These are usually highly motivated people who are eager to serve.

**Meet your volunteers somewhere fun!**

The beach, the lake, the state park, the bowling alley, or laser tag are just a few suggested places where you can have fun with your leaders. This type of team building cannot be over-emphasized. It provides people the opportunity to meet and spend time and interact with someone in children's ministry they do not know, and it purposefully builds healthy relationships within your ministry. A key is to schedule these regularly and make it worthwhile for your leaders to attend—because they are going to enjoy it.

In doing this you

are creating a

broader net to

catch new talents

that are out there.

### Find out, what are their likes?

Send out an email to do a quick inventory of your leaders' favorite things such as food, candy bar, soda, flavor of ice cream and find out their birthday, anniversary, or their favorite holiday. Then place these on a spreadsheet so that you can surprise them in the hallway one Sunday with a small treat that they will love.

### Create a book club.

This is a fun way to go through leadership material. Set up a book club. Choose a book to read through together. Set a time and place to meet on a regular basis. Rotate assignments on who leads and shares, and who brings food. (Did I mention food was important? Yes, it is.) Always have a snack at meetings. People need something to do with their hands, and enjoying food together is a strong part of fellowship.

### Periodically poll the leaders.

Leaders want to be heard. Ask them for their input. It is simple to send an email with just one question and you will be amazed with the feedback. Sometimes they will even offer to help when you had not even gotten that far! Often I found that if I had been praying for this new venture (and every new venture should be bathed in prayer) God would direct my conversations and email. That is an example of leading from the heart!

### Provide fun, purposeful quarterly trainings.

Children's leaders enjoy finding out ways to enhance their classes, ministry, or small groups. Create a fun theme with food, decorations and fun door prizes. This will make your leaders feel appreciated and valued. It will also give your leaders ideas that they can use. Choose topics or presenters that will benefit all age groups. For example, a workshop on special needs or First Aid and CPR. These add value to the lives of your volunteers.

### When change is coming let them know.

Whenever I initiated any change in our children's ministry I would always have an orientation. I would include demonstrations using the new materials and show samples of books and resources. This gave everyone time to process and take ownership of the change. Everyone needs to prepare for change. Do not overlook this important step.

### Let them bend your ear and care for them.

Volunteer leaders want to be heard by you, so listen. That means in the lobby, stay focused on their eyes when they are talking to you, and keep a notepad or index cards with you to write down what they need you to know and understand. Encourage your leaders (remember this is all volunteers) to send you an email so you could read it the next day when you are less distracted. When they have a need, spend time caring

**Choose topics or presenters that will benefit all age groups.**

for them. Bring them dinner, visit them in the hospital, help them find a service or a provider when they need a certain skill set. Offer them prayer and encouragement. Sometimes what they really need the most is someone who will just listen to their hurts. The empathy that you give provides a genuine connection with that volunteer. That is providing pastoral leadership. By the way, you can do that even if you are not "the pastor." Remember, we are all ministers of the gospel and serve as shepherds in the name of Jesus.

**Be ready to speak the truth in love.**

The right fit is important. Do you have volunteer leaders who are well-meaning but seem to miss the point? Sometimes the very best thing to do to develop leaders is to help them find another ministry or a better ministry fit. It may hurt at first but you are doing the right thing. This will end up as a blessing for the ministry of your church. The truth is that not everyone is cut out for children's ministry. Sometimes you have to pray people out of children's ministry and help them find another place to serve.

Keep in mind that each volunteer leader is a masterpiece of God's creative hand. Each leader has a multitude of gifts and abilities to contribute and those who are the right fit will be valuable to children's

> The truth is that not everyone is cut out for children's ministry.

ministry. Encourage your team members to sign up for discipleship classes that focus on helping them discover their unique qualities.

Even though I grew up in the church, I don't recall any teaching about spiritual gifts. It was not until I was in college that I even realized what they were and that I had some. This discovery should be offered to children and students in every local church. We are doing our people a disservice if this is not accessible to them. Check out Word Action's Young Believer's Discipleship Series for elementary children. There is a booklet that provides a way to teach children about spiritual gifts. It is called *So . . . What Are Your Spiritual Gifts?* (CD-3210). A free downloadable leader's guide is available at wordaction. com. The leader's guide includes a checklist-style inventory to help children identify areas of strength and interest.

There are several spiritual gift inventories available online to help your leaders discover their spiritual gifts. You can also purposely develop disciples. Many denominations have discipleship programs and materials available for developing leaders. If your church does not offer an intentional discipleship process you might be interested in resources offered by Pastor Rick Warren on line at purposedriven.com.

## Discussion Questions:

1. What would be your favorite way to connect with new volunteers?

2. What fun event could you host that would help encourage your volunteer leaders to get to know each other better and get to know you better?

3. How could you cross-pollinate with other ministries in the church to make this happen?

4. Think back to your very first volunteer ministry. What did you enjoy about that?

# THEY WANT DISNEY ON A DIME
## CREATING FUN ENVIRONMENTS THAT LEAD CHILDREN TO CHRIST

## CHAPTER 5

"When Jesus saw this, he was indignant. He said to them, 'Let the little children come to me, and do not hinder them, for the kingdom of God belongs to such as these.'"
—*Mark 10:14*

There is probably no other passage that gives us greater support for children's ministry environments than this passage. The writers of the synoptic gospels of Matthew, Mark, and Luke, chose to include this in their narratives of the life of Jesus and His ministry. How does this relate to the space that you use for ministry? A boat load!

It was said that Walt Disney (the man) was fanatical about the appearance of his theme parks. No one who has traveled to Anaheim or Orlando (in the U.S.A.) would debate that. When I lived and served in Orlando I marveled at how this man's vision was fleshed out. Quality entertainment for families was the "watchword and song" of this corporation. It simply oozed from the property the moment you stepped foot on it. As I got to know Disney employees personally, I learned of very strict guidelines for dress, personal grooming, and even conversation. It paid off. My first experience with Disney was at 18 but it was still very fresh at 28 as a resident of central Florida. I was transformed back to childhood, just like the commercials on television when I walked out of the cone shaped front car of the monorail train. I was hooked! I had no idea I was going to have as much fun as my two preschoolers. So what made this experience something to savor and more? The environment was designed intentionally for its purpose. The message of Disney movies and characters was woven into every nook and cranny of the park. From the people who picked up the trash with their broom and dust pan to the mouse himself—they all were one with their environment. Their environment spoke volumes before the first song or conversation was had.

**The environment was designed intentionally for its purpose.**

What do the walls speak in your church to the families with children walking in the doors? Or even the families without children! If you are preparing for your first assignment this is a huge question to ponder. If you are currently serving perhaps it's time to look at your space with fresh eyes. Let's imagine that you are building a new facility (now this can happen . . . I did not just take a detour to fantasy Island) and you have been given the task of deciding the look of this space. Let's use the Disney framework to evaluate your existing or new structure.

## The "D" (Disney) Questions to Ask

**D1.** Get on your knees to gain the perspective of a child.
What does your space look like?

**D2.** Is your space clean and fresh?

**D3.** Is the space colorful and kid-friendly? (Paint is cheap and can do a lot of good! Fighting the beige/off-white battle in your church is worth the bloodshed!)

**D4.** Do the children see themselves in the space? (Are there toys, objects of interest, activities they relate to such as sports, adventures, or hobbies?)

**D5.** Is your purpose and message coming through? Remember that environment and actions speak louder than words and brochures.

Messages to consider:

- Children are welcomed here

- Children are valued
- Children are important to us
- We want children to have fun
- We want children to know God's Word

Other things to consider:

- Start with your nursery. Get on your knees. What is the environment saying to you? Is it safe? Use the five "D" questions to evaluate the nursery and early childhood environment.
- Get two or three parents to walk through the spaces with you, and then have them answer the five "D" questions.
- Invite an interior decorator to create a proposal for you on simple cosmetic changes. If you have the finances, create a proposal for age level appropriate furniture, window and floor treatments.
- Contact local schools or investigate your local church for talented artists that could create murals that would reflect your theme and God's Word.
- After you have evaluated and gathered information, create a written proposal and a presentation to share with your pastoral and lay leadership. Help them to catch your "Disney" vision. This simply means designing a space for purposeful and

fully developed ministry to children and their families.

- Be prepared for feedback and offer various plans that can incorporate options for time lines. Sometimes you can't do it all at once. Take things one step at a time, prioritizing the work.

- You may want to first seek assistance from people within the church. As you look to volunteers in your church, make sure that their commitment level is as strong as their talent. Nobody wants a project going on for months at a time, or stopping midstream. However, you will also need to work with vendors and companies outside the church. Remember that when you are working with vendors, companies, or even ministry resources outside your congregation to make sure that you seek approval for these conversations and the details of what the offers entail. The companies may say they will come and just look and offer their input. Some may even offer "free" estimates. BE CAREFUL of hidden costs! Some companies, especially, those whose clients are predominately commercial business customers, will have surcharges and fees for their phone calls or initial visits.

I am not coming down on these business leaders. I just want to offer words of caution. You may simply be doing research but to some "their time is your money!" Once I was doing this very thing. I was collecting bids for design options for our family production stage set, when to my great surprise a bill for $5,000 came in the mail when we chose someone else for the project. I believe in supporting professionals and treating their services rendered respectfully. I just made the mistake of not getting clarity on what they considered a "free estimate." While there are cautions to using outside sources, there are also benefits of using outside sources.

Many church friendly companies exist now to help you create these new environments. They can and will deliver this "wow" factor for you. They use commercial materials that are long lasting and give you a great finishing touch. Some things you will need to understand is that this will elevate your budget on remodeling or construction because the materials and time are not cheap. They will give you: **3D objects** that are pre-constructed and brought in and placed in your area. **Artwork** that is professional. (The company known as Wacky World offers creative wallpaper options for murals and designs.) **Greater detail** with colors and materials that you find at theme parks. **Greater durability** than materials used in low budget decorations or VBS. (I have seen some amazing things done with cardboard and paint but it does not last long.) **Collaboration** with experienced designers and artists for ministry space.

Things to think about:

1. Do you have a purpose for your space?
2. Do you have a theme?
3. Does your space need a makeover?
4. Do you have the support of your pastor and key leaders?
5. Would children and their families be impacted in a positive way?

Do not fall into the trap of thinking that "they want Disney on a dime." I have been there. It is not a good place to be. Rather, take this to the Lord for His guidance and direction. Call two close friends in ministry and run it by them. Meet with your pastor(s) and cast this vision. God provides! We know this but sometimes we are not willing to put the time and energy into the grunt work of getting everyone on board. That is so critical to the success of revitalizing your ministry environments.

**Do not fall into the**

**trap of thinking**

**that "they want**

**Disney on a dime."**

For inspiration and ideas go to the websites of churches that have virtual tours of their ministry spaces. Or if there are churches within your area that have revitalized their spaces, ask to take a tour. Take a look at what they did. Then adapt it to your local church's needs and finances. There may be an artist and builder sitting in the worship service next weekend who may say, "I'm in!" It has literally happened like that before.

**So pray, get your vision ready to be portable, and then see what God will do!**

The other day a friend from Colorado called me and said, "Andy, guess what? Our church leadership board just approved nearly $100,000 for the children's ministry space remodel and upgrade." That was great news! I celebrated that with my friend and colleague. He had done his homework, was prepared, and shared his vision. How exciting it will be for the whole church to get into this and celebrate kids with this project. This will renew their commitment to families with children.

Finally, consider the words of Romans 8:28, "And we know that in all things God works for the good of those who love him, who have been called according to his purpose." Pray this prayer as you consider the environment that God has called you to provide for the children to whom you minister.

## Discussion Questions:

1. Is something holding you back from creating a fun environment that lead children to Jesus? If so, what?

2. What has caused the success or failure of the past?

3. How can you get your church community excited about revitalizing this area of the church?

4. Have you made this a matter of prayer? Have you given the Spirit of God an opportunity to be heard by you and your fellow leaders?

# IT'S MORE THAN JUST ABOUT KIDS
## PARTNERING WITH PARENTS

CHAPTER

6

**"Teach your children to choose the right path, and when they are older, they will remain upon it."**
*—Proverbs 22:6, NLT*

This may burst your bubble but this scripture is not speaking to you unless you are a parent. The writer's audience is the parents. It was not meant to exclude you but to make you aware that you are not the Old Testament's first pick as the spiritual leader of the children in your church. The parents hold that role.

I know now that people tend to parent the way they were parented. After spending years of reading every parenting book known, I have come to one conclusion—you cannot parent effectively without the Lord and His Church. So there is some good news and bad news about this. Let's start with the good news.

**What's good.**

Parents will bring their children to church. For over 20 years I watched this movement. People who have chosen not to darken the door of a church building for years come when they have children. They discover they are over their heads or remember going to church as a child. When these memories are positive, good memories, they head out to church again with their children in tow.

**What's bad.**

Please let me clarify that bringing your kids to church is not bad, actually it is wonderful. The bad part is that what often happens is these visitors are coming and dropping them off in hallways and doorways and subconsciously turning over the spiritual development of their children to others. In other words, they have subcontracted their teaching of the faith to their children to this staff of volunteers within the church. I am not against age level appropriate teaching and environments. Nor do I suggest that everyone should crowd in the auditorium or the sanctuary for a sermon. So are you ready to burn me at the stake for ripping apart your ministry? Let's approach this from another perspective.

Have you ever been frustrated on a weekend when you have given it everything you had during children's church and Sunday school? Perhaps that frustration comes when you are in the foyer of the church, and you overhear a conversation that goes something like this:

**Parent:** So, what did you learn in church today.

**Child:** Nothing.

**Parent:** *(Trying to help stimulate the child's memory)* Are you sure? Well, what was your favorite part?

**Child:** The snacks and lemonade that we had. Oh, and Billy let me see his new action figure. Did you know his action figure can cut girl's hair?

If you are like me there is a feeling of frustration and discouragement that comes over you like a dark cloud. Now I know that children will say the same kinds of things to parents coming home from school but things aren't really that much different there either. So what do we do with our western civilization that has made room for parents to hand off teaching and development to "the professionals?" The answer: partner with parents. Get them connected, involved, and on board with your children's

**The answer: partner with parents. Get them connected, involved, and on board with your children's ministry . . .**

ministry in a way that makes every parent feel supported and equipped by your ministry. First let's take a look at some jargon that is currently running through ministry so that you can avoid any *Band-Aid Approaches* in your thinking and how you strategize. *Band-Aid Approaches* are quick fixes that can easily be corrected with further research, better planning, and vision casting.

### Band-Aid Approach #1

Add the word "family" to your title and ministry name. This is a current trend that creates a slot so that everything will fall into place. There needs to be a strategy for how you minister to the whole family. A name change alone will not do this.

### Band-Aid Approach #2

Hold family worship once a month where the kids attend the main worship service. This works great for giving children's ministry leaders some time off but does very little to foster parent and child conversations. My observations have caused me to conclude that parents tolerate this more than find it helpful.

### Band-Aid Approach #3

Intergenerational means we do the same thing but with everyone there. To have a good intergenerational experience means there is planning and coordination. There is value for everyone involved. No

IT'S MORE THAN JUST ABOUT KIDS

one leaves the experience feeling like they had to give up something.

## Band-Aid Approach #4

Family worship and a shared experience is all we need. This is wrong. Family worship and shared experience is a good thing and an important thing, but cannot be effective on its own. Parents need a variety of tools to help them lead their children and develop them spiritually. Your strategy needs to include spiritual disciplines, conversation starters, easy to use multi-media tools, and the inclusion of both printed and digital literature.

I have marveled at the iPhone and iPad commercials where the marketing centers on showing the consumer all the ways that these devices can be used. It is so true that we no longer just use a phone to make phone calls. The message is simple, "There is an app for that." It just flows right off your tongue like a phrase from a Dr. Seuss book. It is simple. It is easy. They have connected their product with the audience. Imagine what would happen if families that come to your children's ministry saw your ministry more like "Oh, look I have an app for explaining why it is important for my kids to tell the truth. Hmmm. That would be honesty, right?" Instead of just "OK, here is my child's name tag and I keep the claim check so I can get them back."

What are some of the apps you could consider? Let's explore some of these growing trends in family ministry.

Think Orange (Rethink Group). This is a philosophy that encourages churches to see that parents have more time and influence over children than the church community. If red stands for parents' influence and yellow represents the church's influence, then together they make a great amount of orange. Or to put it simply, "more than either could do on their own." You can learn more about this philosophy at rethinkgroup.org.

Faith Begins at Home. This philosophy encourages a more practical approach to creating programming in the local church to reflect time for the family to be at home using church generated tools and resources that enables discipleship to flourish. This could have a great impact on how you and your leadership team schedule and plan your church year. It begins to open that question of how much time could the church encourage its people to take to make room for spiritual growth? There are clear strategies presented for creating a church where family time is just as important as family ministry.

The D6. This philosophy encourages the church to re-examine the commands from the Lord that are found in Deuteronomy 6:7-9. In Jewish tradition this became a practice for people to take little containers of wood and write these verses and other parts of the Torah on pieces of paper and tie the box to the forehead or forearm. This became known as the *tefillin*. The term "myzuzot" referred to door frames and little containers. The D6 movement promotes leaders to center their ministry philosophy on this scripture passage like a rubric for measuring ministry and practices. It does not suggest one method over the other but sees all family-focused ministry as "game-on."

Now I want to lean in and speak very specifically to you about these philosophies. Here is what you need to know. **They are only philosophies**. What that means is that they are designed to guide you in your thinking and understanding, not to dictate what you do. I like to think of it this way—

Suppose you are a painter. You know that an artist will paint a canvas before they frame it. Well, a philosophy is kind of like a large picture frame with a blank canvas in the middle. It provides guidance and direction but gives you the space or opportunity to paint the canvas. Your ministry is that canvas. In other words, **make it your own!** A ministry leader friend of mine often would say in his workshops "ministry by imitation is mockery." Don't just copy it—take a philosophy, even when it is fleshed out in a curriculum, and make it your own. If you do not like to write, find a writer in your church who has educational experience and empower the writer to work with you. Public school teachers are often looking for something different to do in the summer. Let them go at it.

One way to encourage partnering with parents is to create experiences where the parents and their children come to the same place for equal participation. Not a service or worship venue but simply a place where the whole family is engaged. A church in Shawnee, Kansas does a great job of creating what they call "Family Fun Night." Here parents and children come to play together. It has been proven that children at early ages learn so much through play. In adulthood we tend to forget that for ourselves. Parents can learn through play too. The evening is generally centered on games and activities that require family members to work together for a common goal. Here competition is a good thing! (Of course some parents may have to use a little self-control.) At the close of the evening everyone gathers and the children's ministry leaders award families their trophy that in the past, have included designs using plungers, bananas, and other unique objects with engraving. These trophies are displayed with pride in their homes.

There was a philosophy behind this. The lead children's pastor at this church worked very closely with the senior pastor to develop a philosophy they called together "The Family Table." Every event, every program that was created was placed against this philosophy of intergenerational ministry. For example, if the adults were collecting an offering for building churches in a world area the children took part in that project. Age did not separate, instead it was celebrated. The young learned from the old. And this was also true for the old learning from the young.

One thing to be aware of as you minister to families, is that today not all of our children who come through our church doors are fortunate to have two parents. Sadly, there are many parents who feel lonely and isolated because they are doing their parenting alone. This is another area where your children's ministry could be a real hero for single parents. A growing trend is the number of single dads in our communities. Encourage your leaders to be on the lookout for tired or overwhelmed single parents that may just need a listening ear. Often they have no one to really talk to. I am not suggesting a hotline but maybe a conversation over a cup of coffee where you are actively engaged in listening and praying with them. Consider networking to find other parents who share similar interests, hobbies, or same age children. This can do a lot for creating balance in parenting.

**This is another area where your children's ministry could be a real hero for single parents.**

Many families were picking up their children at the close of the venue on a Sunday afternoon. I was in my typical "end of service location" greeting and saying good-bye to children and their parents. There were the usual "high–fives" and "See ya later" expressions. You know the type, the kind that make leaders feel real good all the way through despite the busy work week that has just ended. As I concluded with my interactions, beginning to think about lunch, and what was coming up next, I saw them coming. They were one of the last clusters of people on their way out the door. As they approached I could see a high level of energy not just coming from the children but also exuding from the father of this little tribe. Joe, a single parent in our church, reached out to shake my hand and asked with a big smile on his face, "Pastor Andy, would you come over and visit us? I mean, do you make house calls?" I smiled as I pictured in my head the stories of doctors who knew their patients during a time when there was such a thing as house calls. "Sure, I would love to," I said. As my response was heard by this family a mini-celebration erupted in the hallway. All three children jumped up and down with the thought of their children's pastor coming to their home. I asked Joe to call my assistant and gave him some options from which to choose.

When I arrived back in the office the following week, I discovered an email with the date of this interesting house call. I thought this would be a typical visit like several I had made throughout the years. Boy, was I wrong. When I pulled in the driveway I was greeted by the whole family on the porch. I was pleasantly escorted into a modest ranch-style home, and offered a beverage. While three young children waited patiently, their father proceeded to share from his heart. He told me their story, about a divorce that was very unpleasant, his company being overwhelmingly supportive of single parenting, and the most incredible thing of all, how our new format in children's ministry had changed their family life. Joe went on to reference take-home materials, our monthly virtues, the family service we recently had started, and the powerful conversations that they were having every week as the lessons they learned were coming home with them.

As I was receiving all of this, my heart was stirred as I thought of the many team members that had given so much over the last two months as we had begun new endeavors. During a very personal tour by the children of their rooms and play time areas, I was reminded of why I am a children's ministry leader, and was humbled by the opportunity to do something that had eternal purpose. We hear a lot about single moms in our culture today, but very little is said about single dads. Here was a great success story of how God used a tragedy, a company, a community, and a children's ministry to transform sadness into joy. Where could you find a greater performance evaluation of a ministry? People are our product and this dad genuinely gave our ministry a glowing compliment because he saw real changes happening in real life, on a day-to-day basis. May we all strive for this kind of excellence.

Another way to create tools for parents is to offer parenting seminars. Schedule a series of these through a month or during summer events. Keep them informal in a relaxed atmosphere. Look at people in your community, school district, or even parent magazine groups that will come and present at your church. Often these are very knowledgeable people, who are eager to have a place to share. Possible topics that you could cover with a series of sessions:

- Children and Technology
- Bipolar Disorders and Other Special Needs
- Discipline
- How to Deal with Bullies

Make sure you interview your speakers in person or by phone before you give them this speaking opportunity. They need to be respectful of God's Word and the theology and ministry of your church.

**Look at people in your community, school district, or even parent magazine groups that will come and present at your church.**

Finally, have information regarding counseling services in your community that you can refer parents to that need specific therapeutic services. If you are not a licensed therapist, do not try to be one. There are many dangers in attempting to offer advice beyond pastoral counseling. Having a list of Christian counselors in your community is a great resource to hand a parent in need. Find out what your church's policy is on counseling and how they choose to support that type of ministry to parents.

Children's ministry is more than just working with children. It is a ministry that can touch all the members of the family in a powerful way. Try to encourage your church leadership to embrace a family ministry philosophy that will disciple whole families.

Finally, when considering ministry to families, if your community is like mine there are many more families at the soccer field on the weekend than at church. Soccer is a good thing, no issues there. To make church as much of an effective experience as soccer requires some planning and cross-pollination of the whole church. Where do you begin? First, start praying. Ask the Lord for guidance. Then begin holding conversations with your church leadership. Ask questions. Share your philosophies. Offer recommendations

**To make church as much of an effective experience as soccer requires some planning and cross-pollination of the whole church.**

on strategies where the church's resources could be best used. In the words of the boy Mikey, who did not like eating cereal for breakfast, "Try it, you might like it!" It can be scary to branch into new approaches, but it can also be well worth the effort and growing pains.

## Discussion Questions:

1. How is your children's ministry currently impacting your parents?

2. What tools do you provide parents with to teach the faith?

3. What are the conversations you need to have with your pastor about children's ministry?

4. What do you see as the benefits for "living out" a family ministry philosophy?

# AN "OTHERS FOCUSED" CHILDREN'S MINISTRY

## CHAPTER 7

"Let us not become weary in doing good, for at the proper time we will reap a harvest if we do not give up. Therefore, as we have opportunity, let us do good to all people."
—*Galatians 6:9-10a*

Jeremy was the children's pastor of a very active church in his community. Jeremy had started serving in the church as a teenager, and then during his second year in college he was asked to lead the children's ministry. He was honored and brought excitement to the church. The kids loved him. Jeremy had a great relationship with the children and their parents and his team of volunteers. As the months went by Jeremy began to feel tired, run down, and discouraged by the ministry role he had been given. He sat at his desk in the church office and looked at his calendar, and then realized that he had five activities and events coming up in the next two weeks in addition to several meetings that he was required to attend. Jeremy was beginning to wonder if any of this activity was really reaching any kids or just keeping the same group of kids active and busy. Jeremy discovered that he had a lot of cool stuff happening but it was not creating a way to reach non-believers. Jeremy felt trapped.

It seems like a simple idea and yet it can become the very last thing we get to. Or worse it only becomes a priority two or three times a year. Can you guess what I am referring to? Reaching kids! Not just for bait, to get their parents, but a genuine, intentional strategy to connect with kids and provide a way for them to experience the love of our Lord.

Perhaps you have struggled for a long time with your role as a children's ministry leader when it comes to what you are actually accomplishing for the kingdom of God. Hundreds of churches struggle with this very question: Why do we exist?

Before we answer this question together let's consider that you may have fallen into one of the following traps. They are easy to get into but can be more difficult to get out. That is because it usually requires change in habits, behavior and philosophy. In other words it could be painful. So let's examine these together—do you see a trap where you are?

### Trap #1

*A program offered once a year will take care of this.* The church leadership wants a

Vacation Bible School. Understand this is a good thing but often this is where the expectations stop. There are many examples of where a traditional VBS has been used effectively to reach children and even entire families in the church community. If that is the case then I applaud your hard work and ministry. Unfortunately, in many cases this is more of a trap because a church will buy a VBS starter kit, pass it to a kid-friendly person and say "take care of it."

A few faithful volunteers respond and come each night only to disappear by the weekend. In some cases children return to the church they had so much fun at the following Sunday only to discover that VBS is over and many have gone out of town for the weekend. How disappointing this is for children that were introduced to Jesus by the faith community, but return to find the members of this ministry team have "checked out" and miss the excitement of a new believer coming to know Jesus as Lord and Savior. In some cases children's ministry takes the "summer off" so the children that do return have no one to connect with and that fun environment they experienced is completely gone.

**Trap #2**

*We have to have a midweek program because that is when the choir meets.* For me this is a difficult place to be when one ministry is dictated to by another. Again,

**How disappointing this is for children that were introduced to Jesus by the faith community but return to find the members of this ministry team have "checked out."**

in some communities a midweek program is very effective and meets the needs of families and if that is the case I say "way to go! Keep at it!" However, there are places where this format is not reaching kids and needs to just simply stop. Your ministry will always have a certain custodial aspect to it. After all children do need to be cared for but this should not be the driving force determining what you do to reach children.

### Trap #3

*We will hold an event on a Saturday morning and people will come.* Unfortunately, this "build it and they will come" idea is great for movies but doesn't cut it with the busy families in your community today. The event needs to reflect the activity and lifestyle of the community in which you live and serve. Look for natural connection points, holidays and times when families love to come together. The top three: Halloween, Christmas, and Easter. Try doing something that really resonates with families. Better yet visit your local mall or town center and see what families are doing on a weekend. One barometer would be this: what do they stand in line for? What are they spending money on? These answers should inform you when choosing the right event or ministry plan.

### Trap #4

*This will be something that we can throw together because it is just for kids.*

Your best resources should be put to use in creating a great outreach ministry or event. Families today have very high expectations for recreation and for what they spend time doing. Make a list of all the things you want the attendees to experience from the moment they walk in. This is going to require coordination and meetings with church departments to make it a team effort. You will be amazed at the effectiveness that you will experience if you share your vision for the event and get everyone onboard. Remember, there is power in team.

Earlier I asked the question: Why does the church exist? The purpose of the church is to reach people and disciple them. The church is to be a place of love, acceptance, and forgiveness. So what I am trying to say is that it is not about the members, it's about others. If your children's ministry is to be others focused, it has to be free to develop outreach opportunities that will actually reach children. This can be accomplished through specific, planned single events or ongoing ministry or both.

Imagine if you could focus on one event or ministry. You sought God's direction and He gave you a vision for what that event would be. Now the question comes into view: How do you do it?

When you begin working on your event here are some things to begin thinking through:

- Create a proposal that shows the purpose and goals for the event. Leaders like to see how this will connect with the over-arching vision of your church. They are more inclined to support your efforts if they can see the kingdom benefits.

- Create a budget that will show what you are projecting to spend on the event. Give as many specifics as you can. Try to keep from using large general categories like "supplies." The more specific you are the better you can gauge what your real needs are. The planning always pays off.

- Look for merchants in your community that will donate foods and supplies to your community event. If the event is free they tend to be more supportive. Emphasize that this is a "community event" designed to benefit the community.

- Give a tentative schedule for the event including set up and tear down time. This will help everyone understand the time and space needs in the building and the amount of time for which volunteers are signing up.

- Create a list of what your volunteer needs are and make them available for the church community to sign up. Be specific regarding task and time allotments so people can choose where they would like to help.

- Prepare a marketing plan inside and outside the church. Use all the free community advertising through the newspaper and radio and other community resources. People still get their information from the newspaper, not just the web. See what your community zoning polices are for banners, yard signs, and temporary signs, before spending the money to make them.

There have been whole families who have been impacted by events and ministries of this nature. You may only have one family that comes back to attend worship but that is one family that may have been disconnected from God. That is the point of putting the time and energy into events in ministry that will reach people. That is being others focused. That is being purposeful in reaching people.

It was a personal delight to be given the opportunity to do this in a local church. I was very blessed to have leaders who encouraged me to be creative with these events. For a couple of years we held what we called "Breakfast with Santa". A local rescue helicopter pilot offered to fly onto the church campus and bring Santa from the North Pole. Now, before you raise your eyebrow and think "uh, what does that have to do

**That is the point of putting the time and energy into events in ministry that will reach people. That is being others focused. That is being purposeful in reaching people.**

with the real reason for the season? Dude, it is supposed to be about Jesus!" Well, you would be right. However, the planned **purpose** for this event was "to connect with the unchurched"—remember? Santa is something they connect with and it gives us the opportunity to invite them to church, to be a place where they can discover that "real reason." It is not a soft sell but a warm invitation and brings people because we are reaching out to where they are, so instead of waiting in line at the mall they came to church.

This may not be the kind of event or ministry that works for you. You may receive an even better idea from the Holy Spirit to reach out to others. I would encourage you to pray, listen, meditate on Matthew 28:19-20 (the Great Commission) and follow the Spirit's prompting for what will be the most effective for you and your community.

My hope for you is that you will have the opportunity to experience this kind of ministry in your local church. It is fun. It is personally rewarding to have children come back because they loved the atmosphere of your event. They loved the atmosphere of your church. They have now a fun environment that will lead them to Jesus. Who wouldn't want to be a part of that?

## Discussion Questions:

1. Have you ever looked at your ministry calendar and evaluated your events for the purpose they serve?

2. Do your events connect with the people in your community?

3. How would your current ministry or event reach people?

4. What would be one change you could make to free you up to focus on others?

# YOUR BEST TEACHING TOOLS
## THE HOLY SPIRIT AND YOU

## CHAPTER 8

**"Since we live by the Spirit,
let us keep in step with the Spirit."**
*—Galatians 5:25*

As a child I remember attending services on Sunday evening. The service was identified as the evangelistic service. Years ago people would bring their friends and neighbors to church on Sunday evening because that was the typical free time that most farmers and workers had. The service would begin at 7 after cows had been milked and other chores on the farm were completed. Then the family car was loaded up and to church the people went. What was a typical order of service were several hymns and choruses. Some were in the hymnal and some were just sung by memory. Placed as an interlude to the hearty singing was my favorite part of the evening, the testimonies.

I sat with great expectation as church members would stand and share their story of how Jesus saved them. Usually, it was not a dramatic story but simply a remembrance of how Jesus saved them from sin. Sometimes there was a humorous detail that everyone enjoyed. These became the stories that created the fabric of our church family. When I would sit and listen to these stories I felt connected to the people. Something would always stir in my heart as I carefully listened to the speaker.

**There is a lack of communication between the different age groups of people in the body of Christ.**

Over the years there was an emphasis on creating separate environments for age groups. Age-level appropriate ministry was gained but what was lost was the sharing of stories of faith between the generations. The seasoned walk of the mature believer is now an absent piece in the repertoire and not being heard by the young and the new believers. There is a lack of communication between the different age groups of people in the body of Christ. What has been lost? The art of spiritual communication—the skill of learning how to share what Christ has done in your life that caused a radical change, transformation, and hope.

What I am about to say may cause ministry resource leaders and vendors to twinge but I have to say it. Here it comes: *the greatest teaching tool that you have is your story!* There, I said it. I do not want to minimize the value of having ministry tools. Just looking at my shelves in my office would make me a hypocrite if that was the case. I love the creativity that children's ministry leaders have. I love going to exhibit halls and finding something new to teach with. Today we're so blessed to have an industry filled with great tools for getting the job done. But there is no tool you can acquire that can take the place of your personal testimony. This story or testimony can make a huge difference in the connection with others. For centuries the major teaching tool was story. History was only communicated orally until the advent of the printed page. It is a natural human expression to share a narrative with others. The problem is that we do not create those intergenerational opportunities where the stories are heard and this art form is taught to the young believers. Here are some thoughts to help you model this important tool:

- Have a good attitude about sharing. Don't make the mistake of thinking you do not have a story. You do!
- Don't assume that the children are saved. Even children that attend church regularly may not have made that decision.
- Choose a portion of your story that is age-level appropriate. There is no need to create confusion. The

**But there is no tool that you can acquire that can take the place of your personal testimony.**

younger the audience the more simplistic you will need to be.

- Offer time for feedback and questions. Children love to ask questions when they are processing. It helps them to relate better the more they can relate your story to theirs.
- Choose a portion that relates to where kids are.
- Have resources available for parents to follow up with whatever takes place at church. Communicate with your parents what has happened for their children! (please hear that!)

Stories do not all have to be about conversion experiences. You will find that the stories that stick like glue to children, students, and adults often are the most simple but very real experiences that create a common connection between the story teller and the audience.

You will find it amazing what happens in your relationship when children in your church discover that you were caught lying or did a "naughty" thing as a child. It makes you more real to them. You become human and relatable to them, and not just a leader. It provides hope for them that the Lord will help them grow just like He helped you. Often I have used this story in children's ministry:

*When I was seven years old I was helping my uncle and aunt move. They had* just graduated from college and they were moving from their third floor walk up apartment in Quincy, Massachusetts to a home in a rural community in Indiana to begin ministry there. As you can imagine, a seven-year-old can quickly and easily get bored with moving boxes from an apartment into a moving trailer. So I did what every seven-year-old might do—I made up some fun. At the door going upstairs was a set of doorbells for the apartments. There were three buttons to press. I pretended that they were the door openers for me to go through like a secret passage. So I pushed them going up and I pushed them coming out. I was enjoying my new made up fun until just the moment I was returning up the stairs and pushed the doorbell. This time the door on the first floor swung open with lightning speed to reveal a very tall, hairy guy who looked at me and said very loudly, "Hey kid, did you press my doorbell?" I looked up at that moment into the man's dark angry eyes and said what any kid might say in a situation like this, "No sir, I didn't do it." Then I walked away to load another box. As I turned the corner there was my grandmother looking right at me. I froze. She did not look happy. I knew that look. Then, the two words that I knew once they were spoken, it was all over

*—the gig was up—"Now Andy!" she said. I heard the words. "Yes, Grandma?" I replied. She took my hand into hers and said very calmly, "Why don't we go for a walk." We placed the box in the moving trailer and began our walk. Grandma proceeded to share with me that she had heard what I said and told me she was disappointed that I had lied to the young man who lived on the first floor. She went on to explain that the young man might have been sleeping because he worked the night shift or maybe he was not feeling well. Grandma explained to me that lying was a sin and I should never be afraid to tell the truth. She explained to me that I needed to ask God and the young man to forgive me. We went to a street bench and sat. There I asked God to forgive me with my grandmother looking on and embracing me for support. When we arrived back at the doors to the apartments I rang the bell one more time. In a few moments the door opened with the appearance of the same hairy man with the same angry face. My knees were shaking but I looked up at the man and said, "Mister, I am really sorry. I rang the bell. I am sorry I lied to you. Please forgive me." The man's eyes softened a bit and he responded, "Well, OK, just don't do it again." The door closed but my heart*

*was open. That was the day I stopped ringing strange doorbells but it was also the day I learned the value of honesty.*

When you tell a story like this you are opening the door for the Spirit of God to work in the hearts and lives of the listeners. That is why "your story" is the best teaching tool. It is also appropriate for you to extend an invitation to your audience inviting them to have Jesus become their Savior and cleanse them from their sins.

## Your Co-Teacher: The Holy Spirit

The work of the Holy Spirit is a mystery. After years of reading about the characteristics of the Holy Spirit, let's face it, the Spirit is a friend, coach, and counselor, but unique all at the same time. He remains a mystery but present and involved all the same.

You can rest assured that as a believer you never walk into that classroom or ministry opportunity alone. You have the power of the Holy Spirit to guide, direct, and push you forward. This is not regulated to just senior pastors and missionaries but is a constant source of power for each person that God calls to proclaim the Word.

My friend Pat Verbal is a gifted and talented communicator and leader. I have watched her lead children to Christ and lead other leaders in their development.

Here is what she says about the Holy Spirit and you.

*"You have an awesome co-teacher, the Holy Spirit. His job is to transform children into the image of God's Son, Jesus. That transformation starts when they accept Jesus as Savior and Lord. Only as children yield to the Holy Spirit can He change their characters so that the children you teach see His exquisite fruit in your life and desire it for themselves."*\*

Pat goes on to offer five ways in which the Holy Spirit works to bring boys and girls to Jesus.

1. **He equips teachers with the ability to share the gospel.** (Ephesians 4:11)
2. **He gives power to the message, using it to speak to the hearts of the children.** (1 Corinthians 2:13; 1 Thessalonians 1:5)
3. **He helps boys and girls see their need of salvation.** (Luke 15:7; Acts 2:37-39)
4. **He creates within them a desire to turn from their sin, to trust Christ, and to start living a life that will glorify God.** (Luke 15:20-21; Acts 11:18)

---

*\*Taken from a CMT workshop, Helping Children Take the Hand of Jesus, written by Pat Verbal and printed by International Network of Children's Ministry, Castle Rock, CO. Used by Permission.*

**5. He sometimes calls believers to devote themselves to special ministries in evangelism.** (Acts 13:1-2)*

When I had the opportunity to lead a children's ministry training event in Nairobi, Kenya I had the honor and privilege to share with over 80 children's ministry leaders these two very important concepts: the power of story and the work of the Holy Spirit. It was amazing to see how much that inspired people who had traveled for three days from Uganda, Ethiopia, and Kenya to come and listen to that training. It was only a couple of weeks later when I read an email that shared reports of how men and women were using these tools to radically transform their children's ministry in their local churches.

If only we could advocate more of this kind of philosophy in our very materialistic/consumer environments of North America. What would happen if leaders got really honest about their ministry and their leadership influence and focused more on the transference of story through the work of the Holy Spirit? Would we see a great number of people, children and their families renewed, reborn and transformed for Christ? I wonder.

What would happen if leaders got really honest about their ministry and their leadership influence and focused more on the transference of story through the work of the Holy Spirit?

## Discussion Questions:

1. Have you ever told a child your story of meeting Jesus?

2. How could you better plan those times of more informal conversation where stories could be shared?

3. What could change in your direction for ministry if it was more Spirit led?

4. What is mysterious about the Holy Spirit to you?

# THEY WILL KNOW IF FUN IS A CORE VALUE!

CHAPTER

**". . . for the joy of the Lord is your strength"**
*—Nehemiah 8:10*

A children's ministry leader called me one day and said, "Andy, our kids have stopped coming to children's church. The parents are telling us that their kids are bored with their time in church." I replied with a suggestion that I would visit and give this leader some feedback. When the day of the visitation took place I arrived and was greeted by my friend and spent the morning observing the environment, the volunteers, and the children. There were some very good things happening but as I conversed with people I started seeing what my friend had been sharing earlier. Everyone was doing their assigned tasks. There were clean, attractive rooms and a pleasant atmosphere but there was an essential element that was truly missing. Fun.

In the past fun was not permitted to be listed as a core value because it did not come across as educationally sound. There was an underlying current that said, if they are having fun, they must not be learning anything. In church ministry somehow we accepted the fact that if the kids colored a paper and recited a scripture verse then everything was in good form. Did you know that there are children in your church that dislike coloring? They interpret that kind of activity as passive and they are looking for more intellectual activity to stimulate their mind and imagination.

**Did you know that there are children in your church that dislike coloring?**

Here is some of the feedback that I gave to my friend:

- Limit the amount of time children sit around the table. Don't make that the entire session.
- Create learning centers that will give children options when they come in the door and at the end of the hour.
- Offer a couple of creative make and take options besides crayons. (Crayons are fine but there are so many other low cost options that will increase creativity. Sand art, water colors, bingo blotters are just a few).
- Dress-up stations for spontaneous role-playing.
- The use of drama in a large group setting that blends sketches and small group discussion with leaders.

Children are not just entertained but they are learning through real life experiences and conflict resolution being played out.

- Take some of the instructional time outside under trees (this church had fabulous green spaces).

In God's Word there are over 40 references to joy. A hot spot for these references are in the book of Nehemiah. Most of us can recall the story of Nehemiah. What comes to mind is how God used him to rebuild the wall of Jerusalem, his strategies for leadership, mobilization, and diplomatic relations. What are often not on our minds are the many examples of how Nehemiah led the people to have and embrace joy. We skip over this part of the story because we so often have failed to see the value in planning fun.

"Nehemiah said, 'Go and enjoy choice food and sweet drinks, and send some to those who have nothing prepared. This day is sacred to our Lord. Do not grieve, for the **joy** of the LORD is your strength.'" *(Nehemiah 8:10)*

Nehemiah wanted God's people to share the joy. Spread it around.

"Then all the people went away to eat and drink, to send portions of food and to celebrate with great **joy**, because they now understood the words that had been made known to them." *(Nehemiah 8:12)*

Nehemiah brought the joy to the people through the knowledge and power of the Word of God.

"The whole company that had returned from exile built booths and lived in them. From the days of Joshua son of Nun until that day, the Israelites had not celebrated it like this. And their **joy** was very great." *(Nehemiah 8:17)*

Nehemiah made room for anyone who came and the joy was compelling.

[*Dedication of the Wall of Jerusalem*] "At the dedication of the wall of Jerusalem, the Levites were sought out from where they lived and were brought to Jerusalem to celebrate **joy**fully the dedication with songs of thanksgiving and with the music of cymbals, harps and lyres." *(Nehemiah 12:27)*

Nehemiah made way for the ministers of the people to serve and fulfill their calling in and through the joy. Joy was created by people who were using their God-given gifts.

"And on that day they offered great sacrifices, rejoicing because God had given them great **joy**. The women and children also rejoiced. The sound of rejoicing in Jerusalem could be heard far away." *(Nehemiah 12:43)*

All ages of people were welcomed and became a part of the joy. No one was left out. They all were a part of the joy. It was a part of their worship and everything they did.

**Joy.** Imagine if these passages from Nehemiah 8 and 12 were reflective of your children's ministry. What would happen to the *climate* in which you serve? Who wouldn't want to come and be a part of it? There would be little resistance from volunteers. They would find that this was their favorite hour of the week. **The fun that would be so visible as a result of the joy that was being shared; it would be contagious.** Irresistible!

My concern about the children's ministry I see as I visit many local churches today is that convenience is a strong core value. You see, when I am talking about fun, I am speaking of the result of a well-planned, executed, and biblically enriched experience. Let's shatter some myths about fun in ministry:

**Myth #1:**

The only way to have fun is to play games. You know the culture at your church the best. Find out the interests of your children and plan activities that they will enjoy. But they do not have to be all

The fun that would

be so visible as a

result of the joy that

was being shared; it

would be contagious.

Irresistible!

games. Once I created a small group elective for kids on Wednesday nights called *Tools of the Trade.* This gave kids the opportunity to learn various trades and to use the tools that are associated with each trade. An example of this is a woodworking class where the kids used real tools to make wooden bookends. Another one was a cooking class. They were fun, interactive, hands-on, and promoted scripture memory and applied biblical truth to the skills they were learning.

**Myth #2:**

The girls don't mind sitting a lot. It is only the boys that must be active. This kind of gender bias should be left in the 50s but unfortunately it still exists today. Girls need more than passive learning. They too need interactive and creative movement for their spiritual growth. Keep your ministry gender balanced in the activities that you plan.

**Myth #3:**

In order to have fun I must use a DVD based curriculum with short segments to teach children at church. The mistake that many people make when they purchase a box, can, or DVD case is to expect the curriculum to do all the work. Multimedia can never replace dedicated, creative, warm, caring volunteers who are passionate about reaching children for Christ. Many of these series are well-written and have some excellent methods and material but do not be tempted to simply "plug and play." Keep your team engaged in interacting with children.

**Myth #4:**

I have to have snacks. Snacks can bring a sense of comfort and peace to any environment. It's one of my personal favorites while leading a group of preschoolers. Boy, were they good listeners to my story of Jonah and the whale while consuming cheddar-flavored, goldfish-shaped crackers. All I am asking is that you are careful not to make this the center of your plan. Branch out and use food for a variety of activities. To this day my teenage children still remember candy-coated chocolate candy during math class at school.

My friend Larry Orwig a former human resources executive for a large company in the Baltimore area, introduced me years ago to a guideline for evaluating an event or activity where people would be involved. He called it: K.I.S.M.I.F. **Keep It Simple, Make It Fun.** I have kept that in my head over the years when planning. The larger the ministry the more this concept was crucial to the implementation.

This helped creative teams get from the brainstorm level to the reality level. It was always amazing to me how some personalities could be very creative but they did not take any ownership for the project or lesson. Ideas would just leap off the page but often would land with a "thud" when it did not fit this K.I.S.M.I.F. rule of thumb. That is why it is a good idea to keep creative people and detailed people around you to help take your creative ideas and make them a reality. That creates fun for everyone without creating conflict and overwork for just a select few.

Give yourself permission to try something new. Sometimes I have surprised myself with how much I enjoyed silly string or shaving cream when appropriately used in ministry. Hah! Did that sound crazy or what? Of course I loved it! Who wouldn't? Creating fun is a real perk to the work we call children's ministry. Go for It! Give it a try and you may learn that it is not the best thing to do, and that is OK. Some of my best learning experiences in ministry were failures. "Well, I won't do that again!" If you have fun then your leaders and children will have fun too. Why? It is because you are creating an environment, a community of fun, of freedom to smile, laugh, and experience the joy of the Lord.

**Give yourself permission to try something new!**

## Discussion Questions:

1. What causes leaders to hold back in their pursuit of fun activities?

2. How could you make learning God's Word fun?

3. Name one person who made learning about God fun for you. What did they do that makes you remember that?

4. Pray and ask the Lord, "Where are the areas of my ministry needing some joy?" Look for ways to incorporate fun.

# IS YOUR CHILDREN'S MINISTRY A SAFE PLACE?

## CHAPTER 10

"People were bringing little children to Jesus to have him touch them, but the disciples rebuked them. When Jesus saw this, he was indignant. He said to them, 'Let the little children come to me, and do not hinder them, for the kingdom of God belongs to such as these. I tell you the truth; anyone who will not receive the kingdom of God like a little child will never enter it.' And he took the children in his arms, put his hands on them and blessed them."
—*Mark 10:13-16*

Church Investigated for Mistreating Child
Interim Pastor in Place Due to Abuse Allegations
Youth Pastor Had Sex with Teen in Youth Group
Childcare Center Closed Due to Abuser Cover-up
Associate Pastor Terminated for Misconduct with Children
Sunday School Teacher's Home Searched for Child Porn

Lifted from the headlines of our newspapers across the country are the tragic and unthinkable things that have occurred in the last place people would suspect abuse to take place—the church. I recall how scared I was the very first time I had a police investigator show up looking for a background check and screening information on a day program for preschoolers' employee who had been suspected of dragging a child across the room. The family's medical doctor had seen what appeared to be carpet burns and it went downhill from there. No matter the accusations, there is nothing more seriously damaging to a children's ministry or church than child abuse and sexual abuse.

Christ made it crystal clear and it appears in all three synoptic Gospels—children and their well being matters to God. For the language of the New Testament to be so clear with the words "do not hinder them" speaks volumes against the backdrop of a culture where women and children were not visible, valuable, or listened to in the culture of the time. This is another example of how Christ spoke love and wisdom into the minds of the people to create a new line of thinking for the day—children are significant and have worth. This lines up with the Jewish importance of teaching and training children even from a young age.

This is another example of how Christ spoke love and wisdom into the minds of the people to create a new line of thinking for the day . . . children are significant and have worth.

Your leadership in children's ministry is founded on the trust of the church body. It is absolutely essential that you take this responsibility seriously and not "blow off" the necessary procedures and policies that must be in place. Every church should have the following:

- **A risk reduction policy.** This is the overarching plan as to what you will do and not do. It becomes a list of standard practices that you will put into place. This is the framework for the way of thinking that you will promote in your local church. It will give you the backbone for all the activity you will do. At times it may even defend your actions when someone questions the procedures you have taken. This should be written and submitted to the lead pastor and church board for approval. If your congregation organizational structure of the board has a finance committee they should be a good start, for these are people gifted in discerning policy and procedure. Once it is approved then you can start putting it into place. Encourage yearly updates for accountability. Be sure to include any known expenses that will be required to uphold the policies.

- **A background check.** A database search for known offenders from local, state, and federal sources. Any judgments or convictions will be noted. Anything on file will show up. Pay careful attention to multiple addresses, DUI, DWI, possession of illegal drugs, and other reports that may show poor use of judgment in behavior. If these "red" or "yellow" flags appear, contact the volunteer(s) directly for a face to face meeting. This provides necessary clarification and an opportunity for promoting the need for screening and safety. Once I did a background check on myself and my driver's license came up suspended over a speeding ticket that I had paid. What a problem that would have been if I had been pulled over. Document all meetings and keep notes in a locked file for future investigations if they occur. Note the locked file. This must be secured information.

- **A volunteer application.** This is vital to the screening process. Biographical data, previous addresses, questions about use of illegal substances, convictions or judgments, spiritual journey benchmarks, and the applicant's social security number are all needed. Another important piece is a section where you sign off on approval or disapproval and dates. If there is disapproval, note the reason why. (Your memory is never as good as it needs to be during an investigation.) These details provide the necessary information for processing, and the kind of material that investigators need to see. You may be considered negligent if you fail to retain this information. This also protects the volunteer when this information is documented. These should be kept in a binder for easy access and kept in a secure, locked place. Limit access and treat as you would personnel files.

- **Interviews.** Whether over the phone or in person—have them! There have been times when I felt it in my gut that children's ministry was not a good fit for someone. I was usually right. Those instincts are good. Listen to them. Read body language.

- **The buddy system.** Pair up the new volunteer with a seasoned one. Not only do you provide personalized training but you have another pair of eyes on the scene. This also ensures no one is working with children alone. Team work is just a good idea.

**You may be**

**considered negligent**

**if you fail to retain**

**this information**

- **Bathroom supervision.** Opposite gender volunteers should not be taking children into the bathroom. If your classrooms do not have single accessible toilets, then tag team with another volunteer and straddle the doorway so that you have supervision in the bathroom and hallway. That allows for privacy and safety.
- **Fire evacuation plans.** Check with your local fire department on what requirements you must meet. At some point you may even have to have a fire drill. Of course your coordination with the whole church will keep everyone from a panic. The alarm going off during the service may not go over well without some prior notification. You may even get an insurance rebate if you perform these drills. Check on the need for other safety plans and precautions. For example, do you need to be aware of plans in place for tornadoes?
- **First aid and emergency equipment.** Have a parish nurse or EMT help guide you in getting supplies and equipment in place.
- **CPR training.** This is a very important class that is also a benefit to the community as many professionals need to keep their certification in this area. Advertise the classes and

charge a nominal fee. The American Heart Association is good at offering classes to non-profits and churches for reasonable fees.

- **Environmental safety reviews.** Invite a board member and a parent to tour your ministry area and ask them to review furniture, equipment and space for safety concerns. If your church is used during the week for childcare or school, then work with the school director and make it a team effort. This promotes communication and teamwork for a safe place.

- **Two person rule.** Children are to never be left alone with just one adult or teen in the classroom or ministry area. That way if there is an emergency, children are not left alone.

- **Check in and out plan.** Leaders must be able to account for children at all times. Provide parents with a system to be contacted if there is an emergency. This also prevents people other than parents and legal guardians from picking up children. The larger the church the more vital this is. Name and face recognition is not always possible. There are several systems available to the church that link with the church database to take attendance, generate name tags, and create claim checks for parents to use to pick up children. This is usually a financial investment. If it is cost prohibitive, then use two-part name tags that can be pre-printed and filled in by parents upon arrival.

At this point you are probably thinking, "When am I going to find time to do all of this?" The answer to that is to make time! Some of it can be done with volunteers, but the overall process should be something you keep a handle on. Again, you do not want to be caught off guard. Our world has become an accusatory charged place. The process does not guarantee protection but it will definitely reduce the risk and show your due diligence. The point: you make the effort. The safety and protection of your children depends on your work here. If the church is safe the kids will be that much safer.

Another great plan to have in place is a Behavior Development Plan (BDP). What? Well, we used to call them discipline plans. I never personally liked that name for this because that seemed to have a negative connotation. My predecessor at one church I served in had created a discipline plan that was very well-written and concise. There had been a lot of effort put into this. However, it bordered on negativity. To keep the plan focused on the positive but at the same time have appropriate consequences, look for a way to praise good behavior and encourage the modeling of quality.

Dr. William Glasser in his book *The Quality School* emphasized that children have five needs.

- Power
- Hunger
- Love
- Respect
- Fun

The idea was that if you understood what these needs were you could create an environment where these needs would be met. He suggested to educators that children have rules and consequences, but also have the opportunity to create a plan that would help them meet their needs. The responsibility was placed on the children for how they were going to meet the expectations of the teacher or leader. The children were to be removed from the activity when their behavior was not in line with the rules, and if this happened then they had to write a plan before being able to return to the group. The plan might be very simple like: "I am going to keep my hands and feet to myself by staying in my seat during reading time. I will get five minutes of extra time at recess if I do this."

The idea was promoting that children could participate in the correction of their own behavior. It kept the teacher or lead-

> The idea was promoting that children could participate in the correction of their own behavior. It kept the teacher or leader from being the bad guy.

er from being the bad guy. The plan was signed by the student, teacher, and parent. Now at church there may not be as much time to accomplish all of this, so getting parents involved is essential and necessary for the completion of a plan. You may need to use email or other communication depending on the size and dynamic of your children's ministry.

A great thing to do when you first arrive at a new ministry is call a "town meeting" and create your children's ministry BDP. This could begin with a plan on chart paper or white board that every child participates in creating and signs. This constitutional experience promotes "buy in." Don't leave out consequences! Make sure there is a list of rules but also what happens if the rules are not followed. We called one plan simply "The Growth Plan" and included the name of our church or children's ministry.

The Assertive Discipline movement started by Lee Canter suggested that there be at least three rules and no more than five. That always made sense to me. If you have more than five rules they become a blur and difficult to make transference into the children's life and routine. A sample list would be:

Growth Steps (Rules)

1. Respect Others (and their property)
2. Follow Directions (Pass this to someone)

3. Listen and Respond (Did you hear what was said?)
4. Be a Good Helper (Patient and kind)
5. Make Good Choices (What would Jesus do?)

Next, have three consequences that start out simple and become tougher as they go:

1. Warning (a verbal communication)
2. A removal from activity (Go write a plan on how you can be successful)
3. A walk and talk with the children's pastor or director

A prepared, formatted note was created to provide communication on how each child was doing in the assigned group. It was a simple checklist that would be easy to use and take just a few minutes of the teacher or leader's time.

You will want to meet with all of your children's ministry team members and demonstrate the use of the plan. Make sure they are clear on how to implement the new plan. You want everyone to have buy-in. If only a few are using this, it will not be as effective and will be confusing to children as they move from one group to the next.

Create a written parent communication that you can also place on the website and email when you need to reference it. Here is a sample of how to state the BDP to parents. Be clear and concise.

### CLEAR EXPECTATIONS

Posters in classrooms display our **5** expectations:

*Respect*

*Participate*

*Listen*

*Follow Directions*

*Make Good Choices*

### CONSISTENT CONSEQUENCES

Posters explain the process of behavior modification:

1. Warnings
2. Redirected
3. Walk and talk
4. Parent Conference

### REWARDS (SOME ARE NOW AND SOME WILL BE ETERNAL)

- Weekly OR Monthly

By choice of teacher: (pencils, stickers, small toys, candy)

- Quarterly highlighted/posted praise!

### PARENT COMMUNICATION

Each child will be tracked by their teachers.

A copy of this communication will be placed in your church mailbox on the <u>last</u> Sunday of the month.

Now you are on your way to establishing a safe environment for children where they will be loved and accepted. Feel good about this! Your work will pay off. Just remember that risk reduction is good but not fool proof! There are going to be situations and events that happen in the body of the local church that you will not have control over.

There are times when you are going to be called on to be an advocate for children. This is the reality of leadership in children's ministry. Some of the most heart–wrenching experiences I have had with families were during domestic issues within the family that turned legal. These days family law has become a slippery slope. Once you start down that path it doesn't slow down and inevitably people get hurt. Here are some things to consider: When a child comes to you about the behavior of another child or adult, listen to them very carefully and write down everything. Then call the parents and meet with them to discuss consequences for the behavior. A more controlled setting may be needed for a period of time while the child at fault is receiving counseling or learns self-control. I watched my children's principal do this at our public elementary school. She was an excellent listener. Her notes became the guide to conversations with parents. She interviewed every child that had anything to do with the situation. She was respectful and firm but kind.

If there is abuse involved, do the careful listening as mentioned. Communicate with your church leadership about the accusation that has been made and call the local government agency child protective services and report the facts as they were told to you. Make sure that this is firsthand information. Not only is this a good idea but is required by federal law. As a leader in the church, a professional in the community, you have to report any abuse or neglect that you have been told about or witnessed. A report is processed through the local agency's intake and then an inquiry is made within 24 hours of the call. The agency may need you to send your notes as documentation but that is not required. If the local, state, or federal police contact you for any paperwork or documentation, it should be given to support the investigation. You want to cooperate. Don't wait for the search warrant.

There may be a cause for you to appear in juvenile court as a witness to the character of a parent or the condition that a child has experienced. My words of caution would be to only agree to this if it is beneficial to the safety and protection of a child. That is the kind of advocacy that is worth every effort. Remember the words of Jesus? *Do not hinder them.* That is a direct command by our Lord to protect children. That is what we must do! Pray as you go. Seek Godly counsel from professionals and Christian lawyers. If your church is fortunate to have a member who is a lawyer,

**As a leader in the church, a professional in the community, you have to report any abuse or neglect that you have been told about or witnessed.**

seek out advice and let the person give you guidance on courtroom conduct.

Be ready to encourage parents and children when cases begin. Often it can take months (even years) for everything to be resolved. Be ready to walk this road with families who come to children's ministry because it is a safe place. They will need your reassurance that God has not forgotten them nor turned a deaf ear. Encourage them to stay in God's Word and come to worship even though their human instincts will be to run and hide.

I have been blessed to serve at some wonderful churches and with wonderful people. When I was a young leader just starting out in ministry I would hear stories of places where there had been reports, accusations, and misconduct but never dreamed it would happen in my church. Does this kind of thinking sound familiar to you? Sure. No one wakes up in the morning, comes to church, and wishes anything like what has been described here. I want to encourage you and warn you at the same time. It will happen. Some day you will get a phone call that will blow your mind and someone that you know very well will confess some horrible things to you. You will hurt, cry, and will feel your heart breaking but you are the leader. You must lead. Through the personal pain you must lead your church and ministry by getting to the

**Through the personal pain you must lead your church and ministry by getting to the truth and speaking the truth.**

truth and speaking the truth. Do not cover it up or try to pretend everything is OK. It won't be easy and things will never be the same. However, your leadership can pave the way for God to heal, restore, and renew if you honestly confront and communicate with the church. I discovered this in a very personal way and learned some important things. God did not cause a friend to fail but God used that failure as a teachable moment in my life.

## Discussion Questions:

1. What would be the list of practices and procedures for your risk reduction plan?

2. What does your insurance company, district or local church require you to do?

3. How can you get parents and leaders "onboard" with you?

4. Who has skill sets in your church to help you with this process of creating and implementing practices for a safe church?

# CELEBRATING THE RITES OF PASSAGE

**"Impress them on your children. Talk about them when you sit at home and when you walk along the road, when you lie down and when you get up. Tie them as symbols on your hands and bind them on your foreheads. Write them on the doorframes of your houses and on your gates."**
*—Deuteronomy 6:7-9*

Once I attended a bridge ceremony for a child in our church who was moving from cub scout to boy scout. The movement from one troop to another was a very celebrated and honored transition. There was a banquet where all the dens and troops came together. There was fellowship and the sharing of food. After the meal the leaders conducted a ceremony where boys who had completed all their badges and requirements walked over a footbridge and were greeted on the other side with new pieces to their uniform and affirmation. There was even a leader with a Native American costume demonstrating how white fabric representing the boys would not burn when lit on fire if they were noble and true. (Amazing what you can do with rubbing alcohol!)

What a great ceremony. I enjoyed every part of it. I sat there and thought, "Wow, the boy scouts really know how to show significance to the coming of age." The journey from boy to young man was celebrated but it also did something much more impacting. It reminded the entire community of the value of hard work, discipline, and taught the values and virtues that the community wants to instill in the children. This is one of the last organizations that still model this very ancient and noble custom. After all, before there were groups like the boy scouts, these ceremonies were the centerpieces of the tribe or community with the focus on the family unit. Each family had personal customs and celebrations. Each tribe had significant ceremonies that were passed down by each generation. I guess the social scientist in me thinks "another blessing of western civilization and individualism" has removed some of this tradition.

So what can we do in children's ministry to capture the beauty and honor of this idea of teaching while celebrating? The answer is to establish some rites of passage in the church that will communicate our desire to follow the biblical emphasis of training and bringing up children in the ways of the Lord.

If we were honest about our feelings, there would be a discussion at this point regarding the time and energy it takes to put some of these "moments" together. That would be a correct way to look at this chapter. It will require planning and preparation. If this is not in alignment with your gifting, then find someone who could work alongside you to help carry out the details. You share the vision for these rites, and then allow people who plan and prepare well to make it happen. Here are some examples of some really good rites of passage that have captured the beauty of life, our theology, and biblical historical practices:

- **Expecting Parents** (formally known as Cradle Roll, *Hand in Hand*). Celebrate with these new parents by sending them cards and notes. Meet with them and offer tours of the children's ministry area. Give them some information on how church nursery ministry works and functions. Suggest ways they can pray for and support this ministry. A nursery ministry

The answer is to establish some rites of passage in the church that will communicate our desire to follow the biblical emphasis of training and bring up children in the ways of the Lord.

baby shower where people give a gift to the nursery in honor of their child or grandchild. Make sure you visit them in the hospital when the child arrives to welcome the child and pray for the new family. Simple *baby bundles* can be created by getting someone to make blankets and fill them with a church diaper bag tag and/or a CD of lullaby music. (see resource list—Appendix A)

- **Child Dedications or Baptisms.** It is said that John Wesley would stop right in the middle of his sermons and perform a christening. He would use water and sprinkle-baptize the head of the newborn and teach his congregation about prevenient grace. Wesley celebrated this new life in the church family. Many congregations also enjoy this opportunity to teach the parents about their role as Christian parents and follow the example of Mary and Joseph when they brought Jesus to the house of the Lord (also called temple in that day) to have Jesus dedicated. Parents are guided through the ceremony and charged with the God-given responsibility to teach, lead, and direct their children to a saving knowledge of Christ. Proverbs 22:6 is wonderful wisdom from God that

**The key point here:**

**involve the parents.**

Solomon shares: "Train up a child to choose the right path and when he is older he will remain on it." You may choose to give a red rose or another flower to symbolize the fragile, delicate life that the parents now have in their watchful care. Another good gift is for the children's ministry to provide a children's Bible or Bible storybook that is age-appropriate and durable. This encourages the reading of the Word and developing a sense of God's story of love for humanity. Pictures and certificates are great to give as reminders of this rite of passage for both child and parent.

- **Class Promotions.** This is a great time to invite the congregation into the discipleship process and give children the opportunity to feel special. This can be done in a variety of ways and methods. The setting can be formal or informal. Some churches are open to weaving this with picnics, music presentations, and other special events.

- **Child Salvation Experiences.** I can't think of a more important or significant point on the journey. Please consider throwing out all the stops for this. For years I thought, "Wow, the response to this should be like a birthday party!" So I would make up a special mailer with a bracelet, stickers, and some kind of candy treat. In it I placed a note to the child and one to their parents and included a basic Bible study packet (*So . . . You Want to Follow Jesus?*) that the parents and child could do together. I have seen some great ideas over the years. Some churches will schedule quarterly parties where they have birthday cake to commemorate the spiritual birthday of children and a teaching time for parents and children to review what took place. The key point here is to involve the parents. If you don't, you may unconsciously go against biblical teaching. Parents are the spiritual leaders of their children. As a children's ministry leader you are partnering with parents, remember? Any way you slice it, celebrate what God has done in each child's life. By doing that, you are modeling the concept to your parents and church. It makes coming to know Christ more contagious and fun!

- **Church Membership** (*id. Nazarene Membership for Kids* is an example). As children approach upper elementary and the preteen years they are eager to learn more about

**As a children's ministry leader you are partnering with parents, remember?**

their own spiritual relationship and their part in the body of Christ. They are no longer satisfied with being spectators but are excited about the possibilities around them. Boys and girls are ready to make those bold first steps outside their nuclear family and act more independently in their thinking and in their behavior. A natural place for them to test their "wings" is the local church. Be ready to offer discipleship and membership classes beyond the core program and schedule. You may want to introduce a series or opportunity to the entire preteen age group, grade group, or children's church but be careful to make this time appealing and in harmony with family schedules. You may want to shy away from school nights if at all possible. Many denominational groups have curriculum for use for this age group. Recently I had the opportunity to help create this format for the Church of the Nazarene, and a very up-to-date and fresh collection of resources were created (see appendix A resources). Here are some good ingredients to use in making a discipleship experience for this age group.

- Keep it simple and have snacks

- Keep it to one hour and make it easy to understand
- Keep it visual and hands-on
- Keep the parents in the loop by asking them to join you for the final session and give them tools to engage with the kids

Topics could range from Articles of Faith such as the trinity, salvation, sin, free will, and sanctification to church history and what a person does to stay a healthy believer. In the next chapter we will get to discipleship experiences where we will break this down further. Children who are candidates for church membership should have already:

- Had a specific salvation experience to which they can testify
- Been baptized (although that is not a requirement but a suggestion)
- Clear understanding of communion
- Understand what a healthy church needs to stay healthy
- Have the permission of their parents to join the church

The membership sessions should be a balance of church history and the Articles of Faith with an emphasis on commitment to the local body, its beliefs, and practices. Make sure you emphasize the connection with the Church of Jesus Christ and the work and core values of your denomination.

The work in the local community is important and needs to be seen as a place to "bloom where you're planted," but there is also value in combining the strengths and resources of the global church in order to reach more people around the world. Helping children to see the local church vision and the global mission is a great way to help them digest this kingdom principle. Imagine if Paul had stayed in Antioch and never ventured past the six-mile radius of his local faith community. That sure would have cut back on his writings in the New Testament. Not to mention, change the church of today.

Once the children and parents have gone through sessions like this go ahead and schedule a date to have the senior pastor meet with the children who are candidates for membership. Plan early on a time where the whole congregation can witness this membership induction. Give the church body time to greet the new members and offer congratulations. One year I had the children who joined our local church and denomination create science fair type displays. We posted them in the lobby. After that venue where they were inducted, they went out and stood by their project display and people came to greet them and they showed off their projects. The kids beamed with delight when people listened to them as they shared. (Hint: Doing those in-house

**Helping children to see the local church vision and the global mission is a great way to help them digest this kingdom principle.**

during the class with supplies and a computer and printer helps a lot!) This was not just a show. Right there in front of my eyes were kids who that day were becoming further woven into the fiber of that local church.

- **Movement to the Student/Youth Ministry**. Remember that story about the cub scout becoming a boy scout? There is nothing sweeter and more meaningful to a children's ministry than to see children make that passage from one ministry to the next in the same local body. You see, the smart student pastors (and I have met many) know that where there is a strong and healthy children's ministry there will be an awesome youth group. I am all for student ministry reaching out and winning people for Christ. However, to have a group of strong believers enter and create a foundation for that outreach is incredible.

  So the student pastor and I would work together and create a ceremony that highlighted the passage of children into student ministry. There is a 12-week module series called *wired!* that is designed for this transfer. (See Appendix A.) It began with the children's ministry highlighting the collective spiritual achievements of the preteen group. (Sometimes it was 5th grade moving to 6th grade, other times it was 6th grade going to 7th) Here is one of the summaries:

The Preteen Journey (All 15 of the Preteens)

15—Know Christ as Lord and Savior

3,754—Children's Church Experiences and Sunday School Classes

14—Members of the Church

15—Baptized

15—Attended at least one camp or retreat

9—Bible Quizzers

12—School Honor Roll

2—Boy Scouts

27—Sports Teams in the Community

6—Children's Talent Participants

12—Have invited two or more people to church

12—Tithe and give to Missions

15—Attended five or more Vacation Bible Schools

Then the children's pastor presented them with a Bible or gift and sent them one-by-one over to the student pastor to receive. The children's pastor passed a runner's baton over to the student pastor signifying that he was receiving the responsibility of shepherd for these new students. The student pastor talked about the new adventures and created enthusiasm for sticking with the journey. The preteens left the stage and presented their parents with a rose like the one given at child dedications symbolizing the appreciation for their dedicating them to the Lord and for parenting them throughout childhood.

Over the years research has shown that it is at 6th grade where we lose the most people to the church and its ministry. This emphasis is a start to changing that statistic and creating a greater awareness in the church of this potential pothole in ministry. Let's try a variety of things to keep filling those potholes and not lose children when they come of age and enter middle school or junior high. The needs of this age group are demanding and it requires much work on the part of the church to provide resources for it. Don't give up! If this is where you identify a weakness in your ministry, make sure you pray and ask the Lord to provide what you need to keep preteens engaged.

Finally, have frank conversations with a couple of parents and find out where they see your ministry is in need of a facelift. Is

**These rites of passage can boost not only the image of your ministry but will elevate the "soul care" of your children's ministry away from "you just take care the kids and pass out goldfish crackers."**

it the nursery? Is it preteens? Somewhere in the middle? These rites of passage can boost not only the image of your ministry but will elevate the "soul care" of your children's ministry away from the "you just take care of the kids and pass out gold fish crackers." That will motivate volunteers to join and for leaders to come alongside you and help you lead children on the journey. When others see your heart they will walk with you and put their heart in the ministry. *That makes it become less task-driven and more heart-driven. Then you are leading from the heart.*

## Discussion Questions:

1. How can you create your rites of passage that blend well with your church's style and energy?

2. What area of your ministry could use a face lift?

3. Do you have rites of passage for all the age groups of your church?

4. Which passage could use some refreshing? Visibility?

5. Pick one event a year to add to the spiritual journey of your children. Which one will you pick first? Why?

# CREATING FAMILY DISCIPLESHIP EXPERIENCES

**"For this reason I remind you to fan into flame the gift of God, which is in you through the laying on of my hands. For God did not give us a spirit of timidity, but a spirit of power, of love and of self-discipline."**
*—2 Timothy 1:6-7*

When I was a child, I remember going through my Bible and looking at the pictures that were in between the pages. I must confess that this was often a habit that manifested itself during sermons on Sunday night. I know I was listening to my pastor but my mind would wander and my imagination was stirred when I saw these stories dramatically unveiled as I turned the page. Many children of my generation were visual learners. We were readers but we were conditioned, thanks to television, to quickly process visual information. So for all the publishers that placed pictures in children's Bibles over the years, I say thanks!

Now let's move to another clip from my childhood—family devotions. Regardless of who led this in our family it was a nice time but if I was completely honest I would have to say that it was boring. Very few people I went to Christian college with ever talked about their family devotions. If it did happen to fall into a conversation it was glazed over with lethargic descriptions and discouraging accounts of disinterest. I kind of wondered why this was the case for so many people who were saved at an early age and lived in Christian homes. Why was this pattern so prevalent in people of faith?

In the first chapter of 1 Timothy, Paul is giving instruction to us to "fan the flame." Here he is most certainly speaking to us that the gift of God, our salvation through Christ, our faith and life as a believer needs a "log on the fire" and some "stirring up." This is discipleship. This is the dilemma. We are not bold and accessing the power of the Holy Spirit, in fact we are too timid. It's time to turn up the volume on the heat. Children's ministry leaders need to do just that, crank it up and make some noise about family discipleship.

In our post-modern culture today people have a very negative view of three words:

Disciple   Discipleship   Discipline

If I was to place these three words on cue cards and place the preferred word of people in our community on the other side, when you flipped the words over they would read:

Leader | Quick & Easy | Fun

**Leader vs. Disciple.** We all want to lead. that has a wonderful sound to it, I am a leader. The problem with this is that we are not communicating things in the right order. Yes, I desire all of the children to whom we minister to become leaders. However, leaders must first be followers. The definition of disciple is:

**Dis-ci-ple** (di-'si-pəl)

One who receives instruction from another; a scholar; a learner; especially, a follower who has learned to believe in the truth of the doctrine of his teacher; an adherent in doctrine; as the disciples of Jesus Christ.

In our fast-paced world there is a tendency to move too quickly through this process. Musicians study under great musicians. Artists sit next to their teachers and watch how they hold the paintbrush, designers receive feedback from their coaches on improvements to their pieces. Yet when it comes to our spiritual development no one relates to these analogies. Often responses are no more than "read the Bible."

To become a change agent or catalyst you could provide some ways to motivate parents to see their children as disciples.

**Quick & Easy vs. Discipleship.** Everywhere you look there is an advertisement that uses the words "quick" and "easy." After all, they are the words that catch our eye when we are looking for a way to achieve something or become something. We love the idea of getting it faster, competing with time like the number 1 goal is who can get there first. We complete an academic program in half the time, we choose a diet that promises results, we choose medications, ointments or lotions that communicate the same set of goals. But let me ask you this—would you want to be operated on by a surgeon that cuts corners? How about a diving instructor that had just read the book and bought the equipment but had not clocked time in the water? I know, what about sitting in a seat on an airplane with a pilot in the cockpit who had only piloted a simulator? This takes on a whole new meaning for me when it is placed in those contexts. I want the person providing something for me to know more than the head knowledge. I want them to be able to apply it through skill and experience. The hard road is "less traveled" but at those times there is a high value placed on the journey. So what can you do about this as a leader for positive change?

**Dis-ci-ple-ship** (noun)

The state of being a disciple or follower in doctrines and precepts.

This definition uses the phrase "the state of being." This is usually understood as a condition or period of time, location or place where a disciple is in a learning relationship. Time and place are set aside for this. The word that seems to capture this concept the most is "mentoring." A mentor has a relationship that commits to time and place where the mentor cares more about the mentored than content or accomplishment. One of my favorite quotes from my graduate work in spiritual formation was from the work and writings of Henri Nouwen: "It's more about who you are becoming rather than what you are doing."

Encourage your parents to have time set aside for talking about God. That may be in the car on the way to a soccer game or at breakfast between the cereal boxes. Conversations can produce a myriad of discipleship opportunities. Simple questions like: Who can we pray for today? Has the Holy Spirit put someone on your heart to invite to church? Simple conversation starters can be printed off and distributed to families when they pick up their kids. I love take-home papers. I am not against them. Unfortunately, the busy parent needs it simple and short. Place open-ended questions on magnets for the refrigerator; create

**Encourage your parents to have time set aside for talking about God.**

cards that can be taped to the mirror in the bathroom with a scripture and a set of questions. Keychain tags on key rings have proven effective for all family members to retain and use repeatedly.

**Fun vs. Discipline.** Have you ever had someone make the statement in front of you, "Church is boring for my child" or "We need more fun around here for kids!" Or how about this one, "I am going to have (child's name) sit with us in big church because he says he isn't learning anything he doesn't already know." Have you lost some enamel on the back of your teeth when they grind together? Well, I have, because I would take those statements and process them in my head and heart like this. What is the matter with these people? Let's face it, people (short and tall, young and old) are now conditioned to be entertained. I have spoken about creating fun environments but let's take a closer look at this. The definition of discipline:

**Dis-ci-pline** ('di-sə-plən)

The treatment suited to a disciple or learner; education; development of the faculties by instruction and exercise; training, whether physical, mental, or moral.

There is a root here within us as human beings to rebel against anything that sounds, feels, or looks like RULES. Why? It is our human nature to want to go against rules. This original sin that traces right back to the Garden of Eden is the cause. These tendencies are not new and are not relegated to just children. Adults and teens are susceptible to this component of the human condition.

*"Discipline aims at the removal of bad habits and the substitution of good ones, especially those of order, regularity, and obedience."* —C. J. Smith

This is what I have come to understand in my journey that I want to share with you. If we are going to make an impact on the thinking and behavior of our church, parents, and children this is what they need to see:

**Rules/Structure** ---------------- **Fun/Freedom**

People young and old tend to gravitate to one of these extremes on their spiritual walk with Christ. Depending upon their background, time in the body of Christ, and interaction with various leaders and thought, people use this gravitation to guide them on parenting and leading their children spiritually. This integrates into their perception of what you should provide for their children while at church and what they should do at home in discipling their children. So what is it like on those ends?

**Rules are good**. They are good because they provide guardrails for children to experience health and success because they know how far they can go. You can model this. You can create checklists. It is framework. The problem: you can't exclusively use this and alone it morphs into legalism. Our church history can back up millions of examples of why this does not work. The famous parent line: "Well, just do it because I told you to" comes to mind. So this alone is an extreme that will take your ministry and families down the drain.

**Fun and Freedom are good**. They are good because this is a gift from God through Christ. Salvation provides freedom. Jesus came to free us and was God's fulfillment of the law. It is through this grace and peace that we have freedom as believers. So fun is good. Actually, it is awesome! However, if people stay exclusively with just fun and freedom there will be trouble in how things are understood. The level of transference between a mature believer and a new believer will be shaky at best. This is why Paul urged the mature believers in Corinth to be very careful with how they chose to use their freedom.

*"Be careful, however, that the exercise of your freedom does not become a stumbling block to the weak."* (1 Corinthians 8:9)

So let's bring this back around. If you are trying to create a philosophy in your mind that will guide your leadership that comes from your heart on how to guide your families on discipleship, then help them get this:

Rules/Structure ------+------ Fun/Freedom

## LOVE
### (The Real Discipleship)

There is not one children's ministry or church that is going to tank because they loved too much. Offer your families guidelines and tools. Give them great ideas and framework, but keep that structure open for creativity, fun, and flexibility. The Word of God is a living, growing movement of God in the lives of believers. It even woos unbelievers and leads them to Christ.

My Wesleyan-Holiness theology taught me that this is the way to go! Original sin nature is removed at the time we are sanctified. We become free from the original sin but that is the beginning of the process. On the road of my spiritual journey I grow in my understanding of how my faith and behavior can match up and the Holy Spirit continues to convict and guide me, and His power helps me to have victory over the sin nature.

Professor Thomas Oord called this, in his book *Relational Holiness,* the Adventure Model. His model suggested that we use one thing to guide us on this adventure: **Love.** Love keeps us from moving back to the two extremes that I mentioned. It can keep you and your ministry focused on others and keep

There is not one

children's ministry

or church that

is going to tank

because they

loved too much.

your discipleship in check as it is fleshed out in your ministry leadership.

Your ministry must be strong in the Word but can be taught and caught through a variety of methods and styles. Absolute truth is timeless and is for all people and all cultures. With that understanding, put together a plan for how you will foster family discipleship:

- **Bible-reading tools.** I heard Kurt Warner, a Christian professional athlete and philanthropist, share that he and his wife were reading the Bible together in their family room while their children were present playing. His son walked over to them and asked, "Daddy, why are you coloring your Bible?" Kurt smiled and said that he was highlighting some words that were special to him. They were teaching him something new about God. The Warner children were picking up simple, good discipleship by watching their parents read and use Bible reading tools.

- **Take Home Communication.** I mentioned this earlier. Simple and clear scripture and open-ended questions that guide and direct discussion in the home. Tape them to places in the house and make them handy for use.

- **Daily Bread Scriptures.** There are a variety of scripture devotions and cards that you can purchase or make your own. As a child and in our home we had the bread shaped plastic container with the scriptures on little cards that slid in and out of the bread.

- **Cubes and Balls.** Many vendors sell a variety of 3D tools for evangelism and discipleship. These are great for kids because they can practice communication at home with their family. Practice leading Mom to Christ again and again!
- **Select a Time and Place.** In our home we called it **MAD Time or "*Monday After Dinner."*** At the end of dinner on Mondays my wife Sharon and I would have the kids get their Bibles. We all placed our Bibles on the table after the dishes were cleared, and then a member of the family took a turn sharing a devotional from his or her personal copy. We discovered these really cool devotions in the various children's Bibles and Sharon and I had them too. So when the kids became functional readers and could read independently we had **MAD Time**. I watched how my kids thought they had the "power" and they got to choose what we learned that night. (They thought I was yielding something to them so

it was a big deal.) In some ways it showed me where they were at on their journey and gave me insight to how they perceived the biblical narrative. Each week there was something new and different. Each child brought his or her own personality to the table with the devotion.

- **Neighborhood Bible Clubs.** Not everything has to be on the campus or even in the home of the family. Community centers, libraries, and other groups will often let ministry groups that do not charge, use their facilities in the summer. It gives them a community non-profit avenue and creates positive activities for children while school is out. Some of your families may want to host an activity in their backyard or cul-de-sac. They may need some preparation and guidance but they may easily buy into your vision for reaching people and it creates a discipling time for the whole family. Dad can rush home and Mom could get off early from work and connect with their neighbors.

I read somewhere that Susanna Wesley, mother of John and Charles Wesley, would meet with the children every week and have a set time to discuss the spiritual lessons they were learning. It may also be good to know that Johnny and Charlie were two of twelve kids. Time is a tough commodity for your families but sometimes little reminders of the parents' roles as spiritual leaders of their homes helps.

You may want to consider sharing this strategy with your lead pastor and brainstorming about what the church as a whole can do to communicate this philosophy and create a strategy to emphasize family discipleship. You may come up with some fresh ideas that could really perk up your ministry and create some great growth in how whole families can be discipled and disciple each other.

Shared experiences on the weekend provide great times together where children and their parents laugh and learn. There are materials now that create the family experience and offer music, drama, and interactive time where the family learns a valuable truth from the Bible and sees it applied to real life conflicts.

When I led a team of volunteers to do this, I was thrilled that there was no longer dead silence as parents and children left the children's wing. There was energy and conversation. Have you seen this happen when parents take their children to "big church?" I don't think so. For the first time in my work and ministry as a children's ministry leader I saw it with my own two eyes, the frame had been pulled back, I

**Shared experiences on the weekend provide great times together where children and their parents laugh and learn.**

was seeing the whole family "getting it." The ripples of that were huge. People who did not even have children were coming and enjoying the experience. The talk about the experience was being heard all week long and there was a great anticipation for the next week's experience.

Small groups, large groups, Sunday school, family nights, devotional guides, they are all good. Try them on and see what fits your ministry and your church. Have a plan that is derived out of your philosophy of family discipleship. Your church will be a better place, which will in turn make the community a better place.

## Discussion Questions:

1. What is your philosophy about family discipleship?

2. How could you frame a philosophy and create a strategy for your church that would be a good fit?

3. What are some ideas that you could implement to support this?

4. Based on your venue offerings how would you create a balance between what families can do together on the church campus and at home or in their neighborhoods?

# GREAT CHILDREN'S MINISTRY LEADERS KEEP GROWING

**"Do not love sleep or you will grow poor; stay awake and you will have food to spare."**
*—Proverbs 20:13*

I'm thinking that this verse is one of those that at first pass most of us would say, huh? But the analogy holds when you think of it in terms of personal growth. Sleep implies a state of rest but can also mean unproductive or unfruitful. When we are awake and engaged in activity we produce. We all know that you can't give what you don't have.

Sometimes you just have to park your 21st century brain and reflect about the incredible wisdom of Solomon. I love the passages from 1 Kings, chapter 3, where we hear this incredible story of conversation between God and Solomon. It takes place in a dream. Dreams are a very powerful form of communication. I am always intrigued by the dreams that people had that were recorded in Scripture. Usually they are profound turning points in the lives of God's people. They become a clear message to the believer and confirmation that what they are supposed to do is being directed by our Lord. Solomon, like his ancestors Abraham, Isaac, and Jacob had great conversations that resulted in tremendous blessings from the Lord. Hear the account:

"The Lord was pleased that Solomon had asked for this. So God said to him, 'Since you have asked for this and not for long life or wealth for yourself, nor have asked for the death of your enemies but for discernment in administering justice, I will do what you have asked. I will give you a wise and discerning heart, so that there will never have been anyone like you, nor will there ever be. Moreover, I will give you what you have not asked for—both riches and honor—so that in your lifetime you will have no equal among kings. And if you walk in my ways and obey my statutes and commands as David your father did, I will give you a long life.'" *(1 Kings 3:10-14)*

In the book *The Sacred Romance,* the authors, Brent Curtis and John Elderidge, describe one of the current challenges we face in today's world of hearing the voice of the Lord. They describe the believer of today as someone who pushes away, suppresses or even stifles the voice. We turn the volume down very low so we do not have to hear. We feel better, but just temporarily. So what does the Lord do? You got it, He turns up the volume! Sometimes it becomes so loud you hear it outside your heart as well as in, like a spiritual loud speaker.

Imagine the tragedy if King Solomon had not listened to the voice of God. How would that have changed his life and many others? Those times when we are at a fork in the road with the Lord are huge turning points. We have free will, we can choose, but the Lord makes His voice clear. So usually it comes down to His best for me, or going second best with my choice.

When I was a younger man I had an experience with the voice of the Lord that was undeniable to me as coming directly from the Spirit of God. As I had mentioned earlier, I was called by God to serve Him

**Imagine the tragedy if King Solomon had not listened to the voice ofo God.**

and minister to children when I was a child myself at age 12. So I knew the voice of God. I could hear it and I chose to obey and allow God to guide me. For two years I wrestled with the Lord about a full time ministry opportunity.

I wanted one in a bad way. I was teaching public school at the time and was struggling to serve "two masters," the school and the church. After six years of doing that, it was really wearing me down. There was also the change in my family life. Since I had started these two careers, I had gotten married, moved, and had two children under the age of five. Not a lot of time to develop hobbies working six days a week, two jobs, and a family. Anyway, there is a point to this story—I had started receiving phone calls to come to an interview. That was very exciting but the challenge was that it would require us to move 18 hours away from our families. Moving grandchildren away from their grandparents is not easy! So, I was offered a position and had actually turned down the offer three times. I was sure at this point the pastor who had invited me to come work with him thought I was nuts.

Then it happened. The volume was turned up! I was walking into the school building on the first day when teachers have to report back for in-service and meetings. It was a typical warm, sultry day near the upper Chesapeake Bay. The front doors of our non-air-conditioned school were wide open attempting to collect any level of breeze that might happen to come by. It was in that warm breeze that the voice came to me and spoke so clearly that I thought the school intercom was being used in the delivery. The message the voice delivered was: **"YOU ARE NOT SUPPOSED TO BE HERE!"** (I am not sure if all capital letters, bold font, and one exclamation point does this justice. It was loud!) To this day as I write this I still get chills and goose bumps.

Following my hearing was obedience by way of some phone calls. One to my wife saying we are going! Next to a wonderful pastor who was able to look past the wishy-washy me and see what God was doing all along.

Now we arrive at the best part. I am sure someone had said this. It sounds very profound and I would never even begin to take credit for such a cool thing as this. **Obedience produces growth.** Hmmm . . . was I right? I could feel your awe and amazement as you read this. Seriously, it is true. There is such a spike in your learning curve when you completely jump and say let's do it. Obedience is not easy but the fruit that it bears is an incredible time for harvesting personal development. Leaders

**Obedience**

**produces**

**growth.**

know this and can measure growth in their lives and the lives of others.

The mistake that we often make as humans is to get settled in for a long winter. It works great for woodland animals but is fatal to kingdom leaders. Over the years, I have seen solid men and women of God have outstanding ministry and then coast into a maintenance mode, and then miss out on something new and wonderful that God has for them. Sadly, in some cases there were even moral failures associated with this mode of behavior.

Children's ministry leaders must keep growing. I was blessed to have internships where I was surrounded by people who modeled that for me. I got it! They were teachers. They were pastors, even had some math and Spanish up their sleeves. What I am the most thankful for is that they had a passion for learning new things and passing on that learning to thousands of ministry leaders globally. Based on those experiences, I learned that I needed to keep growing. How have I kept growing over the last twenty years?

**I have attended all of the conferences I could get to.** My very first conference as an attendee was the Children's Pastors' Conference created by the International Network of Children's Ministry (INCM) in Denver, Colorado. In January of 1990, I came with a note excusing me from classes in college. I was 22 years old, with $50 in my pocket to spend, and spent that the first day in the resource exhibit hall. I remember sitting there at a general session when Thom and Joanie Schultz came to the stage and announced that they were going into children's ministry and creating a magazine and resources. Half the room was ready to fall over but we all stood up and applauded. (They had only served student pastors and youth ministry up to that point.) I was motivated and inspired to go back and dive into children's ministry. As many times as I could I returned to CPC and other conferences because I wanted to grow. I wanted to soak up everything I could learn from the ministry veterans so that I could reach more kids for Christ. Workshops, resources, incredible speakers—to anyone who has led a conference in the last twenty years—I say "THANKS." You made a difference in my life.

**I have taught workshops at local and regional training events.** I discovered that I could communicate. (What that means was I could talk for an hour and make it sound like I knew what I was talking about.) These experiences forced me to grow, to read up, and to try new things—and if it didn't work I would never do it again. I believe it was Thomas Edison who said he invented over 500 ways to *not* make a light bulb. I think about some of the stuff I did and wonder

**As many times as I could I returned to CPC and other conferences because I wanted to grow.**

how those churches put up with me? You learn from your mistakes. You learn when you share with your peers your discoveries.

**I have networked.** Everywhere I lived and served I sought out other children's ministry leaders and started the conversation. "Let's get together and have lunch." There was so much to learn from each other. I never walked away from one of those times thinking that I wish I had stayed in the church office that day. I always came away with a new idea to try. Over the years that led me to keep a balance between the churches in our community and the churches in my denomination. Sometimes that balance opened the door to some great opportunities. In one case a year of planning resulted in an eight-night outdoor ministry located in a cornfield across from Hatfield Meats in Hatfield, Pennsylvania. Over 30 Churches came together and we had over 400 children every night. Did I mention that we had to do this with a dirt floor and a tent? That did not stop us.

The Lord gave me wisdom to get on the phone and call up people I did not even know and "cold turkey" converse. That led to a great network of children's ministry leaders and friendships. In recent years this passion for networking brought me to larger levels of leadership. I chair our denomination's children's leadership network. Working with a board of directors

I never walked away from one of those times thinking that I wish I had stayed in the church office that day.

from around the country, who share similar passions about ministry, is rewarding. There are now several great professional organizations that you can join, both in your denomination and some that are interdenominational. Here is what I found out about myself when I joined and became a part of these networks—I grew. I also discovered that I was not alone! There are no islands in the kingdom of God. People are the only island makers. Those who make them usually get stuck there.

**I have read professional ministry journals.** There are great resources now that are finely-tuned-in to the growth of the children's ministry leader. I appreciate the work of these periodical editors who are so diligent to find articles that teach, inspire, and encourage us to grow. They are a great source of growth for us. Sometimes I would even go back and re-read issues years later and think, "Wow, how did I miss that?" These make great sources of leadership development for you and your team. Consider routing them to your leadership team or ordering a bulk number of copies. Several of the companies that produce these offer churches group subscriptions.

**I went to college and graduate school.** The doors and windows have now been flung open wide for leaders to go back to school and grow. The creation of online programs is lifting the lid for working professionals who want to grow. There is nothing like a good academic program to help stretch you. You most certainly grow when you are taking a program with a group of people and have a plan laid out as to what you will read, write, and contribute to the learning community.

I was fortunate to find a way to study in an online community for two years with a master's level program. It was one of the most challenging things I ever did in my life. I had put it off for years thinking that my wife should finish her bachelor's degree first. The night she told me that I should not wait for her and she was behind me 100% I was honored that she loved me that much, but I was bummed because that was the last excuse I had and had run out of excuses. So the next day I went to the website of the university that I had chosen and applied. The next day I got an email that said, "Congratulations! You have been accepted in the MAR program." I took a deep breathe and probably went for the brown lunch bag to breathe slower and calmer. Dude, I was now a grad student. I grew. Thanks to many of my professors and friends who encouraged me.

**I have had mentors.** I was very fortunate to have had several mentors in my life. Mentors do not have to be celebrities, just people who can speak into your life with their gifts and discernment and offer solid biblical spiritual direction and guidance. I have had relatives who functioned as mentors and other ministry leaders who invested time and energy into my life.

Now this may have come off a little too rosy colored for you. You may be asking the question, "Well, I do not have access to all of the things you spoke of in this chapter. What do I do if these doors do not open?"Over the years I have had to learn and understand the dynamics of the church. I love the church. I really do. What I struggle with is how the church often handles leadership development. It is true that during lean times economically there is a desire to cut budgets and make sure that the utility bills are paid and that we live off of a cash-in-hand system of managing church finances.

There is also the reality that conferences and seminars are seen as "plush" and not seen as necessary for staff members. What is a tragedy in many churches is that a staff member has to beg or pay out-of-pocket for growth opportunities and is repeatedly told "next year." Pastors and leaders get so tapped out that their creativity trees are moaning and ignored. So much need exists for pastoral soul care. Time away, training opportunities, marriage enrichment, and conferences help the children's ministry leader get in the boat! Jesus got in the boat. The Bible has an account

**What I struggle with is how the church often handles leadership development.**

of that. He had to get away from ministry demands. You should do that too.

Look for webinars and newly developed web-based resources to create your own conference. Get together with some other leaders who did attend conferences this year and have them bring their stuff and have everyone share what they have learned. Start blogging and create a blog called "Life without a conference" and see how many hits you get. Finally, write some proposals including why and what will you do with this information that can be shared with your lead pastor so that you can inform leadership of the purposes behind the conference attendance.

Bring a consultant into your church and have them do an assessment of your ministry and programs. The consultant may be able to create a larger and louder voice for you when they submit their findings and recommendations. Share with them how you feel restricted and unheard. Give them an opportunity to "buzz the tower" and "shake the trees" to get some change going. The important thing here is to grow!

## Discussion Questions:

1. What has been your greatest source of growth in ministry?

2. Name one new thing you could try each month (for a year) in your ministry and keep a journal of what you experienced. What was your favorite learning experience?

3. What are you looking for in a mentor? Who are you mentoring?

4. What fun ways have you grown even when all budgets are cut and frozen?

5. How can you continue to grow in your current ministry assignment?

# SPIRITUAL FORMATION

## KEEPING YOUR BUBBLES IN THE MIDDLE

# 14

> "One who was there had been an invalid for thirty-eight years. When Jesus saw him lying there and learned that he had been in this condition for a long time, he asked him, 'Do you want to get well?' 'Sir,' the invalid replied, 'I have no one to help me into the pool when the water is stirred. While I am trying to get in, someone else goes down ahead of me.'"
>
> *—John 5:5-7*

I love the fact that I am human. I am sure that you have never read that statement before. I am not saying that I love all of the imperfect things about my humanity . . . disease, the common cold, the aging process. Yeah, there is certainly a lot that can bum you out if you keep going down that list. What I mean when I make that statement is that I love being created in the image of God. I don't want to be God. I just am glad I am part of His family.

**177**

My friend Pat Verbal sent me an email during a very difficult time in ministry and she ended her correspondence with a simple but beautiful quote, *"If God had a refrigerator, your picture would be on it."*

You may find that amusing to think that the Creator of the universe uses a Frigidaire to keep His milk cold. We know that is not true. But the thought of being *that important* to God is the kind of feeling I have when I say, "I love being human." We have forgotten this very important concept that is at the beginning of God's story, he made us in his image. He formed us from the dirt. He created humanity and we were one with God.

He knows us better then anyone else. Those of us who are called into ministry become a very unique bird in the kingdom of God. We become very focused on the mission and ministry of the church but we become very susceptible to "out of balance" behavior when our "bubble" gets out of the middle. Have you ever held up a level when trying to hang a picture or construct something? You take a pencil or chalk line and mark where the middle of level would be. The focus is placed on the tiny bubble that, when it is in the middle, is the signal that your line is level. Too bad there is not a spiritual level that if held over your heart would tell you if you were level or not.

**Too bad there is not a spiritual level that if held over your heart would tell you if you were level or not.**

**178**

Jesus has that ability. He can walk up to someone and essentially say, "Your bubble is way off!" or "You are off center!" He cuts through the stuff of people's lives and sees their hearts. So was the case in the passage from John, chapter 5. This story is called the "Healing at the Pool." The pool was two large rectangular pools that for some unknown reason would have undercurrents and would self-stir. These pools called *Bethesda* in Aramaic were thought to produce healing at the time of stirring. Some had been healed at this time. There was a man who had been at the pool for many years because he was an invalid and could not move from his spot to get to the pools when the water would stir.

When Jesus approached this man at the pools in Jerusalem He knew what this man was really thinking. The man is there with no one to help him. So here is an unpredictable source of healing that can affect only a few people, and this man has no hope of getting healed anyway because he cannot get to the pool. In other words, this is a situation of utter hopelessness and futility. But while the man cannot get to the pool, Jesus can get to him. The man is met by the one who is the stable, constant source not just of healing but of life itself, indeed, of eternal life.

Although Jesus knows the man has been ill for a long time and also knows what

**But while the man cannot get to the pool, Jesus can get to him.**

is in his heart (2:24-25), he nevertheless initiates the contact by asking if he wants to get well (5:6). This gospel stresses both divine sovereignty and human responsibility, and here we see both Jesus' sovereign approach to this man and the importance of the man's own will. This is another of Jesus' questions that are intended to reveal one's heart. What would we say to Jesus if He asked us whether we wanted to be healed of our own illnesses, physical or otherwise? Do we want to be rid of our addictions and other sins? Ten minutes hard thought on this question could lead us to new depths of repentance. It seems like a silly question—of course he would want to be healed. But perhaps the man had grown accustomed to his disability and would prefer the known pain to the terror of the unknown, with its new responsibilities.

What would happen if we all received this kind of heart–check? How would you react to that kind of insight into your life? You may not be paralyzed like this man at the pool but maybe you have another form of disability. Occasionally, we call this burnout or depression. Ministry leaders are like other people in health and help service industries. The rate of professional fatigue is huge. What I have experienced in my own life and seen in others, is that I become so used to being out of balance and unhealthy that I frankly grow immune to it. I fail to no-

I become so dry that when I do get to the river I am overwhelmed. I have become spiritually unhealthy without even realizing it was taking place.

SPIRITUAL FORMATION

180

tice the signs. I become so dry that when I do get to the river I am overwhelmed. I have become spiritually unhealthy without even realizing it was taking place.

During a class in my graduate work in spiritual formation, I was asked to map out my spiritual time line. What were the benchmarks and turning points? What were times of victory and defeat? When did I fall? After completing this exercise I discovered that there were times when I got comfortable with "my stuff" and needed the healing touch of Christ. Thankfully, the Holy Spirit convicted me. What a gift that was to receive. God used mature believers to guide me. I would slowly return back to a place of health and the bubble clearly would rest in the middle.

There was also a new attitude that emerged in my journey to become more Christlike. It was my level of personal expectations. I stopped expecting so much of myself and became more dependent on God. I am sad to say that over the years I had learned to be a control-freak children's ministry leader. I wanted ministry to be perfect. I wanted everyone on the staff to have the same viewpoint and passion for children's ministry. I expected every venture to be 100% funded. I was supposed to have all the answers to every family crisis. Does this sound close to the Messiah-complex to you? A very wise friend looked at me one day and said, "Andy, where is there room for Jesus in your ministry leadership?" I could not come up with an answer. That was the start of healing, of *wanting to be healed*. For the first time and many since then I went to the Lord and said, "I want to get well. I need you!" Usually, that is where Jesus smiles and says, "Now we are getting somewhere; now I can use you!"

I want to be used by the Lord to accomplish His work. His kingdom does mean more to me than title, position, job, and recognition. In fact as I share this with you, I am at another interesting point on my journey. I have been in the desert visiting streams. I have been living in between lands. I have had a time of subtraction before I could see what was the next step on the path of obedience. Here is what I do know. I have loved becoming comfortable in my ministry skin. It has taken twenty years to get to this point. Please do not let that discourage you, but rather encourage you to keep going regardless of the place you are on the journey. Remember that you have been called by God. You can join the priesthood of believers and the God of love is awaiting your choice to follow Him.

Don't wait for someone to carry you down to the pool. Your personal growth is your responsibility as a believer and ministry leader. Your health is just as important, and maybe a little more, than the children

**Don't wait for someone to carry you down to the pool. Your personal growth is your responsibility as a believer and ministry leader.**

and families you serve. Taking a day for personal growth is very important. In the book *The Pastor's Guide to Effective Ministry*, that was part of a pastoral leadership series, William H. Willimon wrote about the life of the minister. He discussed the importance of *soul care* for the minister. He shared how Jesus got in the boat but often we are reluctant to do that. We come fatally close to the level of workaholics or depression before we see the need to step away from the demands of ministry.

Find an accountability partner at your church or in the community that will hold you accountable for not the number of days you work but the number of days you take off. This time can be used to mentor each other. Relational discipleship requires that you make time. When was your last vacation? When did you take a book like this and go off alone, to a restaurant, or park bench, and just read? When did you have a prayer or devotional retreat that had nothing to do with message preparation? When did you take your spouse on a date or spend time with a close friend? Give yourself permission to get well and stay well. Start a new hobby. Take a real joy ride. Keep that bubble in the middle.

The kind of sickness that invades the heart of the minister is much harder to detect. So please don't allow yourself to become lost in the ocean or stuck in a deep hole. Get honest about where you are at with the Lord and invite him to heal.

And remember that these are great days in children's ministry leadership. Doors are opening for men and women to serve and make lasting impressions on the lives of children globally. Learn all you can. Stay informed. Connect with other leaders in professional networks, conferences and in your community. Aim high and seek God for vision and direction. You are not alone. There are many who share this passion for reaching and discipling children. Leading from the heart is very rewarding. I highly recommend it and encourage you in it.

## Discussion Questions:

1. Why is it hard for you to take a day off? What makes it hard for you to get in the boat?

2. How can you use accountability to help you keep level with your bubble in the middle?

3. What are the areas of your life that you need the Lord to heal?

4. What would a personal planning day look like for you?

5. How can you adjust your personal expectations to be more realistic?

Do you want to share with or hear from the author? Contact Pastor Andy at ervincrew5@msn.com

# APPENDIX A
## RESOURCE LISTING FOR CHILDREN'S MINISTRY

**Chapter 1**
Book: *Transforming Children into Spiritual Champions*, George Barna

**Chapter 2**
Book: *Visioneering: God's Blueprint for Developing and Maintaining Vision*, Andy Stanley
Book: *Communicating for a Change: Seven Keys to Irresistible Communication*, Andy Stanley and Lane Jones
Book: *Ladder Shifts: New Realities, Rapid Change, Your Destiny*, Samuel R. Chand
Book: *The 360 Degree Leader: Developing Your Influence from Anywhere in the Organization*, John C. Maxwell
Jim Wideman's Leadership Resources, jimwideman.com

**Chapter 3**
Book: *Leadership Essentials for Children's Ministry: Passion, Attitude, Teamwork, Honor*, Craig Jutila
Book: *Lead the Way God Made You: Discovering Your Leadership Style in Children's Ministry*, Larry Shallenberger
Book: *Leading from Your Strengths: Building Close-Knit Ministry Teams*, Eric Tooker, John Trent, and Rodney Cox

**Chapter 4**
Book: *Simply Strategic Volunteers: Empowering People for Ministry*, Tony Morgan and Tim Stevens
Book: *The Volunteer Revolution: Unleashing the Power of Everybody*, Bill Hybels
Book: *Kidlead: Growing Great Leaders*, Alan E. Nelson, kidlead.com
For use with children:
*Young Believers Discipleship Series*, WordAction Publishing Company®
*So . . . What Are Your Spiritual Gifts?*, Young Believers Discipleship Series, WordAction Publishing Company, wordaction.com
One Way Street, Inc., Children's Ministry Resources for children's ministry and for children to use in ministry, onewaystreet.com
Websites:
wordaction.com (follow children link)
purposedriven.com

**Chapter 5**
Environment Development Ministries:
Real Fake Buildings, realfakebuildings.com

Wacky World, wackyworld.com

Iron Spirits, ironspirits.net

## Chapter 6

Family Ministry Resource Websites:

rethinkgroup.org

faithbeginsathome.com

d6.com

Book: *Collaborate: Family + Church*, by Michael Chanley, Reggie Joiner, Fred Stoeker, and Jim Wideman

## Chapter 7

Book: *unChristian: What a New Generation Really Thinks about Christianity . . . and Why It Matters*, David Kinnaman and Gabe Lyons

Book: *Missional Hearts: Best Practices for Evangelism,* (out of print but available in PDF), usamission.org

## Chapter 8

Teaching Workshop: CMT Manual—*Helping Children Take the Hand of Jesus,* Pat Verbal, *(INCM) International Network of Children's Ministry,* ncm.org

## Chapter 9

Kidzblitz Family Fun Events, kidzblitz.com

## Chapter 10

*Safe Kids,* Blake Caldwell, Ed., *Life Stream* Leadership Resources, Nazarene Publishing House, beaconhillbooks.com

*Safe Place,* Marv Parker, Ed., Christian Publications, Inc., christianpublications.com, 1-800-223-4443

*Reducing the Risk Media Kit—Church Law and Tax Report,* Brotherhood Mutual, 704-841-8066

*Church Volunteer Central* website (Group Publishing Company®) and related screening company used, volunteercentral.com

## Chapter 11

*Hand in Hand,* Cradle Roll Ministry materials, WordAction Publishing Company®, wordaction.com

Diaper Bag Tags for New Parents, Custom Designed for your church, NLS Specialties, Inc., nlsspecialties.com

*So . . . You Want to Be Baptized?, Young Believers Discipleship Series,* WordAction Publishing Company, wordaction.com

*So . . . You Want to Take Communion?, Young Believers Discipleship Series,* WordAction Publishing Company, wordaction.com

*So . . . You Want to Follow Jesus?, Young Believers Discipleship Series,* WordAction Publishing Company, Basic Bible study for children, wordaction.com *id. Nazarene Membership for Kids,* WordAction Publishing Company, wordaction.com

*wired!,* WordAction Publishing Company, wordaction.com

Look online for denominational catechism resources

## Chapter 12

Book: *Relational Holiness: Responding to the Call of Love,* Michael Lodahl and Thomas Jay Oord

The Discipleship Place Website, discipleshipplace.com

*Anytime Devotionals,* contact WordAction Publishing Company, wordaction.com, for availability

*Family Times* Virtue Packs, 252basics.org

## Chapter 13

National Conferences:

Children's Pastors' Conference, incm.org

Ignite Leadership Summits, ignitenaz.org

One Way Street, Inc., Regional Puppet Festivals and International Ministry Fests Training and Resources for children's ministry leaders, oneway
street.com

Catalyst Leadership Conference, catalystconference.com

The Orange Conference, rethinkgroup.org

The D6 Conference, d6conference.org

Professional Organizations:

International Network of Children's Ministry, www.incm.org

Nazarene Children's Leadership Network, ignitenaz.org

American Children's Ministers' Association, acma.org

Kidology, kidology.org

Magazines:

*K!* Magazine, kidzmatter.com

*Children's Ministry Magazine & CMM Professional* Edition, group.com

## Chapter 14

Book: *Confessions of a Pastor: Adventures in Dropping the Pose and Getting Real with God,* Craig Groeschel

Book: *Pause, Recharge, Refresh: Devotions to Energize a Pastor's Day-to-Day Ministry,* H.B. London, Jr.

Book: *Achieving Balance in Ministry,* Anthony J.Headley

Book: *The Pastor's Guide to Effective Ministry,* Neil B. Wiseman, Larry Burkett, Wayne Schmidt, H. B. London Jr., Jesse C. Middendorf, William H. Willimon, Dr. Dale Galloway, Jeannie McCullough, Darius Salter, Dallas Willard, Michael Slaughter, Ron Blake, Jim Pettit, Beacon Hill Press of Kansas City

# Develop Christ-centered families and walk hand-in-hand with them while they lead their children into lives of faith.

*Hand in Hand* will help you and your church connect with parents of 0-3 year olds from within the church as well as visitors.

Included in each *Hand in Hand* packet:
- Welcome home card
- Birthday cards
- Tracking form and visitation log
- 12 helpful age-specific brochures for parents
- Parent's Covenant Certificate
- Baby Dedication Certificate
- And more!

**Hand in Hand**
Embracing Families with Young Children
CD-4000

www.WordAction.com

# Be proactive in keeping Kids safe, not reactive.

Keeping kids safe is vital for any children's ministry. *Safe Kids* will help churches take active steps to put safeguards in place for their ministry.

This manual provides:

- Forms and procedures to screen volunteers
- Ideas for structuring the church building to keep nurseries and Sunday school classrooms safe
- Instructions for training children's workers
- Information you must know to identify potential predators
- Policies for reporting suspected child abuse
- And much more!

**Safe Kids**
Policies and Procedures for Protecting
Children in the Church

ISBN 978-0-8341-2085-3

www.BeaconHillBooks.com

**Do you have a strategy for following up
with a child after his or her conversion?**

This engaging five-week Bible study offers a starting
point for helping disciple new young believers in the
faith. *So . . . You Want to Follow Jesus?* is a tool that will
challenge kids and encourage them on their journey.

**So . . . You Want to Follow Jesus?**
A Five-Week Basic Bible Study for Young Believers
CD-3206
www.WordAction.com